Routledge Revivals

The Healing of Nations and the Hidden Sources of their Strife

Originally published in 1915 in the middle of World War I, Carpenter explores the effects that the war was having on society and humankind as a whole from first-hand experience. In particular, papers focus on the differences between Germany and England, the causes of the war and suggestions for restoration and recovery when the war has ended. Carpenter details all of this in a realistic way drawing on matters such as class to put forward his anti-war stance as well as philosophical approaches to coping with tragedy. This title will be of interest to students of history, sociology and politics.

Routledge Revivals

The Healing of Nations and the Hidden Sources of their Strife

Edward Carpenter

Routledge
Taylor & Francis Group

First published in 1915
by George Allen and Unwin Ltd

This edition first published in 2016 by Routledge
2 Park Square, Milton Park, Abingdon, Oxon, OX14 4RN
and by Routledge
711 Third Avenue, New York, NY 10017

Routledge is an imprint of the Taylor & Francis Group, an informa business

Publisher's Note
The publisher has gone to great lengths to ensure the quality of this reprint but points out that some imperfections in the original copies may be apparent.

Disclaimer
The publisher has made every effort to trace copyright holders and welcomes correspondence from those they have been unable to contact.

A Library of Congress record exists under LC control number: 15014700

ISBN 13: 978-1-138-18427-5 (hbk)
ISBN 13: 978-1-315-64527-8 (ebk)
ISBN 13: 978-1-138-18434-3 (pbk)

THE HEALING OF NATIONS AND THE HIDDEN SOURCES OF THEIR STRIFE · By EDWARD CARPENTER

"The Tree of Life . . . whose leaves are for the Healing of the Nations"

LONDON: GEORGE ALLEN & UNWIN LTD.
RUSKIN HOUSE 40 MUSEUM STREET, W.C.
NEW YORK: CHARLES SCRIBNER'S SONS

First published in March 1915
Reprinted . . . April 1915
" . . . Oct. 1915
" . . . June 1916

CONTENTS

I

INTRODUCTORY

THE following Studies and Notes, made during the earlier period of the present war and now collected together for publication, do not—as will be evident to the reader—pretend to any sort of completeness in their embrace of the subject, or finality in its presentation. Rather they are scattered thoughts suggested by the large and tangled drama which we are witnessing; and I am sufficiently conscious that their expression involves contradictions as well as repetitions.

The truth is that affairs of this kind—like all the *great* issues of human life, Love, Politics, Religion, and so forth, do not, at their best, admit of final dispatch in definite views and phrases. They are too vast and complex for that. It is, indeed, quite probable that such things cannot be adequately represented or put before the human mind *without* logical inconsistencies and contradictions. But (perhaps for that very reason) they are the subjects of the most violent and dogmatic differences of opinion. Nothing people quarrel about more bitterly than Politics—unless it be Religion: both being subjects of which all that one can really say for certain is—that nobody understands them.

When, as in the present war, a dozen or more nations enter into conflict and hurl at each other accusations of the angriest sort (often quite genuinely made and yet absolutely irreconcilable one with another), and when on the top of that scores and hundreds of writers profess to explain the resulting situation in a few brief phrases (but unfortunately their explanations are all different), and calmly affix the blame on "Russia" or "Germany" or "France" or "England"—just as if these names represented certain responsible individuals, supposed for the purposes of the argument to be of very wily and far-scheming disposition—whereas it is perfectly well known that they really represent most complex whirlpools of political forces, in which the merest accidents (as whether two members of a Cabinet have quarrelled, or an Ambassador's dinner has disagreed with him) may result in a long and fatal train of consequences—it becomes obvious that all so-called "explanations" (though it may be right that they should be attempted) fall infinitely short of the reality.[1]

Feeling thus the impossibility of dealing at all adequately with the present situation, I have preferred to take here and there just an aspect of it for consideration, with a view especially to the differences between Germany and England. I have thought that instead of spending time over recriminations

[1] Some people take great pleasure in analysing White Books and Grey Books and Orange Books and Yellow Books without end, and proving this or that from them—as of course out of such a mass of material they can easily do, according to their fancy. But when one remembers that almost all the documents in these books have been written with a *view* to their later publication; and when one remembers also that, however incompetent diplomatists as a class may be, no one supposes them to be such fools as to entrust their *most* important *ententes* and understandings with each other to printed records—why, one comes to the conclusion that the analysis of all these State papers is not a very profitable occupation.

one might be on safer ground by trying to get at the root-causes of this war (and other wars), thus making one's conclusions to some degree independent of a multitude of details and accidents, most of which must for ever remain unknown to us.

There are in general four rather well-marked species of wars—Religious wars, Race wars, wars of Ambition and Conquest, and wars of Acquisition and Profit—though in any particular case the four species may be more or less mingled. The religious and the race motives often go together; but in modern times on the whole (and happily) the religious motive is not so very dominant. Wars of race, of ambition, and of acquisition are, however, still common enough. Yet it is noticeable, as I frequently have occasion to remark in the following papers, that it only very rarely happens that any of these wars are started or set in motion by the mass-peoples themselves. The mass-peoples, at any rate of the more modern nations, are quiescent, peaceable, and disinclined for strife. Why, then, do wars occur? It is because the urge to war comes, not from the masses of a nation but from certain classes within it. In every nation, since the dawn of history, there have been found, beside the toiling masses, three great main cliques or classes, the Religious, the Military, and the Commercial. It was so in far-back ancient India; it is so now. Each of these classes endeavours in its turn —as one might expect—to become the ruling class and to run the government of the nation. The governments of the nations thus become class-governments. And it is one or another of these classes that for reasons of its own, alone or in combination with another class, foments war and sets it going.

In saying this I do not by any means wish to say anything against the mere existence of Class, in itself. In a sense that is a perfectly natural thing. There *are* different divisions of human activity, and it is quite natural that those individuals whose temperament calls them to a certain activity —literary or religious or mercantile or military or what not—should range themselves together in a caste or class; just as the different functions of the human body range themselves in definite organs. And such grouping in classes may be perfectly healthy *provided the class so created subordinates itself to the welfare of the Nation.* But if the class does *not* subordinate itself to the general welfare, if it pursues its own ends, usurps governmental power, and dominates the nation for its own uses —if it becomes parasitical, in fact—then it and the nation inevitably become diseased; as inevitably as the human body becomes diseased when its organs, instead of supplying the body's needs, become the tyrants and parasites of the whole system.

It is this Class-disease which in the main drags the nations into the horrors and follies of war. And the horrors and follies of war are the working out and expulsion on the surface of evils which have long been festering within. How many times in the history of "civilization" has a bigoted religious clique, or a swollen-headed military clique, or a greedy commercial gang—caring not one jot for the welfare of the people committed to its charge—dragged them into a senseless and ruinous war for the satisfaction of its own supposed interests! It is here and in this direction (which searches deeper than the mere weighing and balancing of Foreign policies and Diplomacies) that we must look for the "explanation" of the wars of to-day.

And even race wars—which at first sight seem to have little to do with the Class trouble—illustrate the truth of my contention. For they almost always arise from the hatred generated in a nation by an alien race establishing itself in the midst of that nation—establishing itself, maybe, as a governmental or dominant class (generally a military or landlord clique) or maybe as a parasitical or competing class (as in the case of the Jews in Europe and the Japanese in America and so forth). They arise, like all other wars, from the existence of a class within the nation which is not really in accord with the people of that nation, but is pursuing its own interests apart from theirs. In the second of the following papers, "The Roots of the Great War," I have drawn attention to the influence of the military and commercial classes, especially in Germany, and the way in which their policy, coming into conflict with a similar policy in the other Western nations, has inevitably led to the present embroilment. In Eastern Europe similar causes are at work, but there the race elements—and even the religious—constitute a more important factor in the problem.

By a curious fatality Germany has become the centre of this great war and world-movement, which is undoubtedly destined—as the Germans themselves think, though in a way quite other than they think—to be of vast importance, and the beginning of a new era in human evolution. And the more one considers Germany's part in the affair, the more one sees, I think, that from the combined influence of her historical antecedents and her national psychology this fatality was to be expected. In roughly putting together these antecedent elements and influences, I have entitled the chapter "The Case *for* Germany," because on the principle of *tout comprendre* the fact of the evolution being inevitable constitutes her justification. The nations cannot fairly complain of her having moved along a line which for a century or more has been slowly and irresistibly prepared for her. On the other hand, the nations do complain of the manner and the methods with which at the last she has precipitated and conducted the war—as indeed they have shown by so widely combining against her. However right, from the point of view of destiny and necessity, Germany may be, she has apparently from the point of view of the moment put herself in the wrong. And the chapter dealing with this phase of the question I have called "The Case *against* Germany."

Whatever further complications and postponements may arise, there will certainly come a time of recovery and reconstruction on a wide and extended scale over Europe and a large part of the world. To even outline this period would be impossible at present; but in the sixth chapter and the last, as well as in the intermediate pieces, I have given some suggestions towards this future Healing of the Nations.

The Evil—huge and monstrous as it is—is not senseless, one may feel sure. Even now here in England one perceives an extraordinary pulling together and bracing up of the people, a development of solidarity and mutual helpfulness, a greater seriousness, and a disregarding of artificialities, which are all to the good. These things are gains, even though the way of their manifestation be through much of enmity and ignorance. And one may fairly suppose that similar results are traceable in the other nations concerned. Wounds and death may seem senseless and needless, but those who suffer them do not suffer in vain. All these shattering experiences, whether in a nation's career or in the career of an individual, cause one—they force one—to look into the bases of life and to get nearer its realities. If, in this case, the experiences of the war, and the fire which the nations are passing through, serve to destroy and burn up much of falsity in their respective habits and institutions, we shall have to admit that the attendant disasters have not been all loss—even though at the same time we admit that if we had had a grain of sense we might have mended our falsities in far more economical and sensible fashion.

If in the following pages—chiefly concerned as they are with Germany and

England—I have seemed to find fault with either party or to affix blame on one or the other, it is not necessary to suppose that one harbours ill-feeling towards either, or that one fails to recognize the splendid devotion of both the combatants. Two nations so closely related as the Germans and the English cannot really be so hopelessly different in temperament and character; and a great deal of the supposed difference is obviously artificial and class-made for the occasion. Still, there *are* differences; and as we both think we are right, and as we are unable to argue the matter out in a rational way, there seems to be nothing for it but to fight.

War has often been spoken of as a great Game; and Mr. Jerome K. Jerome has lately written eloquently on that subject. It is a game in which the two parties agree, so to speak, to differ. They take sides, and in default of any more rational method, resort to the arbitrament of force. The stakes are high, and if on the one hand the game calls forth an immense amount of resource, skill, alertness, self-control, endurance, courage, and even tenderness, helpfulness, and fidelity; on the other hand, it is liable to let loose pretty bad passions of vindictiveness and cruelty, as well as to lead to an awful accumulation of mental and physical suffering and of actual material loss. To call war "The Great Game" may have been all very well in the more rudimentary wars of the past; but to-day, when every horrible invention of science is conjured up and utilized for the express purpose of blowing human bodies to bits and strewing battlefields with human remains, and the human spirit itself can hardly hold up against such a process of mechanical slaughter, the term has ceased to be applicable. The affections and the conscience of mankind are too violently outraged by the spectacle; and a great mass of feeling is forming which one may fairly hope will ere long make this form of strife impossible among the more modern peoples.

Still, even now, as Mr. Jerome himself contends, the term is partly justified by a certain fine feeling of which it is descriptive and which is indeed very noticeable in all ranks. Whether in the Army or Navy, among bluejackets or private soldiers or officers, the feeling is certainly very much that of a big game—with its own rules of honour and decency which must be adhered to, and carried on with extraordinary fortitude, patience, and good-humour. Whether it arises from the mechanical nature of the slaughter, or from any other cause, the fact remains that among our fighting people to-day—at any rate in the West —there is very little feeling of *hatred* towards the "enemy." It is difficult, indeed, to hate a foe whom you do not even see. Chivalry is not dead, and at the least cessation of the stress of conflict the tendency to honour opponents, to fraternize with them, to succour the wounded, and so forth, asserts itself again. And chivalry demands that what feelings of this kind we credit to ourselves we should also credit to the other parties in the game. We do cordially credit them to our French and Belgian allies, and if we do not credit them quite so cordially to the Germans, that is *partly* at least because every lapse from chivalrous conduct on the part of our opponents is immediately fastened upon and made the most of by our Press. Chivalry is by no means dead in the Teutonic breast, though the sentiment has certainly been obscured by some modern German teachings.

While these present war-producing conditions last, we have to face them candidly and with as much good sense as we can command (which is for the most part only little!). We have to face them and make the best of them—though by no means to encourage them. Perhaps after all even a war like the present one—monstrous as it is—does not denote so great a deviation of the old Earth from its appointed orbit as we are at first inclined to think. Under normal conditions the deaths on our planet (and many of them exceedingly lingering and painful) continue at the rate of rather more than one every second—say 90,000 a day. The worst battles cannot touch such a wholesale slaughter as this. Life at its normal best is full of agonizings and endless toil and sufferings; what matters, what *it is really there for,* is that we should learn to conduct it with Dignity, Courage, Goodwill—to transmute its dross into gold. If war *has* to continue yet for a time, there is still plenty of evidence to show that we can wrest —even from its horrors and insanities —some things that are " worth while," and among others the priceless jewel of human love and helpfulness.

II

WAR-MADNESS

September, 1914.

HOW mad, how hopelessly mad, it all seems! With fifteen to twenty million soldiers already mobilized, and more than half that number in the fighting lines; with engines of appalling destruction by land and sea, and over the land and under the sea; with Northern France, Belgium, and parts of Germany, Poland, Russia, Servia, and Austria drenched in blood; the nations exhausting their human and material resources in savage conflict—this war, marking the climax, and (let us hope) the *finale* of our commercial civilization, is the most monstrous the old Earth has ever seen. And yet, as in a hundred earlier and lesser wars, we hardly know the why and wherefore of it.

It is like the sorriest squabbles of children and schoolboys—utterly senseless and unreasoning. But broken bodies and limbs and broken hearts and an endless river of blood and suffering are the outcome.

III

THE ROOTS OF THE GREAT WAR[1]

October, 1914.

IN the present chapter I wish especially to dwell on (1) the danger to society, mentioned in the Introduction, of class-ascendancy and class-rule; and (2) the hope for the future in the international solidarity of the workers.

Through all the mist of lies and slander created on such an occasion—by which each nation after a time succeeds in proving that its own cause is holy while that of its opponent is wicked and devilish; through the appeals to God and Justice, common to both sides; through the shufflings and windings of diplomats, and the calculated attitudes of politicians, adopted for public

[1] Reprinted by kind permission from the *English Review* for December, 1914.

approval; through the very real rage and curses of soldiers, the desperate tears and agony of women, the murder of babes, and the smoke of burning towns and villages: it is difficult, indeed, to arrive at clear and just conclusions.

When the war first broke out no one could give an adequate reason for it. It all seemed absurd, monstrous, impossible. Then arose a Babel of explanations. It was that Germany desired to crush France finally; it was that she was determined to break Great Britain's naval and commercial supremacy; it was that she must have an outlet on the sea through Belgium and Holland; that she must force a way to the Mediterranean through Servia; that she must carry out her financial schemes in Asia Minor and the Baghdad region. It was her hatred of the Slav and her growing dread of Russia; it was her desire for a Colonial Empire; it was fear of a revolution at home; it was the outcome of long years of Pan-Germanist philosophy; it was the result of pure military ambition and the class-domination of the Junkers. Each and all of these reasons (and many others) were in turn cited, and magnified into the mainspring of the war; and yet even to-day we cannot say which *was* the main reason, or if we admit them all we cannot say in what exact proportions their influences were combined.

Moreover, they all assume that Germany was the aggressor; and we have to remember that this would not be admitted for a moment by a vast number of the Germans themselves—who cease not to say that the war was simply forced upon them by the hostile preparations of Russia, by the vengefulness of France, by the jealous foreign policy of England, and by the obvious threat embodied in the *Entente* between those three nations; and that if they (the Germans) made preparations for, or even precipitated it, that was only out of the sheer necessity of self-preservation.[1]

Thus we are still left without any generally accepted conclusion in the matter. Moreover, we are struck, in considering the list of reasons cited, by a feeling that they are

[1] As an example of this belief, read the manifesto of Professor Eucken, who represents such a large section of German opinion, and note the absolute sincerity of its tone—as well as its simplicity.

all in their way rather partial and superficial—that they do not go to the real root of the subject.

Out of them all—and after the first period of confusion and doubt has passed—our own people at home have settled down into the conviction that German militarism in general, and Prussian Junkerdom in particular, are to blame, and that for the good of the world as well as for our own good we are out to fight these powers of evil. Prussian class-militarism, it is said, under which for so long the good people of Germany have groaned, has become a thing intolerable. The arrogance, the insolence, of the Junker officer, his aristocratic pretension, his bearish manners, have made him a byword, not only in his own country but all over Europe; and his belief in sheer militarism and Jingo imperialism has made him a menace. The Kaiser has only made things worse. Vain and flighty to a degree, and, like most vain people, rather shallow, Wilhelm II has supposed himself to be a second and greater Bismarck, destined by Providence to create the said Teutonic world-empire. It is simply to fight these powers of evil that we are out

Of course, there is a certain amount of truth in this view; at the same time, it is lamentably insufficient. The fact is that in the vast flux of destiny which is involved in such a war as the present, and which no argument can really adequately represent, we are fain to snatch at *some* neat phrase, however superficial, by way of explanation. And we are compelled, moreover, to find a phrase which will put our own efforts in an ideal light—otherwise we cannot go on fighting. No nation can fight confessedly for a mean or base object. Every nation inscribes on its banner *Freedom*, *Justice*, *Religion*, *Culture* versus *Barbarism*, or something of the kind, and in a sense redeems itself in so fighting. It saves its soul even though bodily it may be conquered. And this is not hypocrisy, but a psychological necessity, though each nation, of course, accuses the other of hypocrisy.

We are fighting "to put down militarism and the dominance of a military class," says the great B.P., and one can only hope that when the war is over we shall remember and rivet into shape this great and good purpose —not only with regard to foreign militarism, but also with regard to our own. Certainly, whatever other or side views we may take of the war, we are bound to see in it an illustration of the danger of military class-rule. You cannot keep a 60-h.p. Daimler motor-car in your shed for years and years and still deny yourself the pleasure of going out on the public road with it—even though you know you are not a very competent driver; and you cannot continue for half a century perfecting your military and naval organization without in the end making the temptation to become a political road-hog almost irresistible.

Still, accepting for the moment the popular explanation given above of Germany's action as to some degree justified, we cannot help seeing how superficial and unsatisfactory it is, because it at once raises the question, which, indeed, is being asked in all directions, and not satisfactorily answered: "How does it happen that so peace-loving, sociable, and friendly a people as the great German mass-folk, as we have hitherto known them, with their long scientific and literary tradition, their love of music and philosophy, their lager beer and tobacco, and their generally democratic habits, should have been led into a situation like the present, whether by a clique of Junkers or by a clique of militarist philosophers and politicians?" And the answer to this is both interesting and important.

It resolves itself into two main causes: (1) the rise of the great German commercial class; and (2) the political ignorance of the German people.

It is obvious, I think, that a military aristocracy alone, or even with the combined support of empire-building philosophers and a jack-boot Kaiser, could not have hurried the solid German nation into so strange a situation. In old days, and under an avowedly feudal order of society, such a thing might well have happened. But to-day the source and seat of power has passed from crowned heads and barons into another social stratum. It is the financial and commercial classes in the modern States who have the sway; and unless these classes desire it the military cliques may plot for war in vain. Since 1870, and the unification of Germany, the growth of her manufactures and her trade has been enormous;

her commercial prosperity has gone up by leaps and bounds; and this extension of trade, especially of international trade, has led—as it had already so conspicuously done in England—to the development of corresponding ideals and habits of life among the population. The modest, simple-living, middle-class households of fifty years ago have largely disappeared, and in their place have sprung up, at any rate in the larger towns, the very same commercial and parasitical classes, with their Philistine luxury and fatuous ideals, which have been so depressing and distressing a feature of *our* social life during the same period. Naturally, the desire of these classes has been for the glorification of Germany, the establishment of an absolutely world-wide commercial supremacy, and the ousting of England from her markets.

"Germany," said Peter Kropotkin[1] a year or two ago, "on entering a striking period of juvenile activity, quickly succeeded in doubling and trebling her industrial productivity, and soon increasing it tenfold;

[1] *Wars and Capitalism*, by P. Kropotkin. (Freedom Press.)

and now the German middle classes covet new sources of enrichment in the plains of Poland, in the prairies of Hungary, on the plateaux of Africa, and especially around the railway line to Baghdad—in the rich valleys of Asia Minor, which can provide German capitalists with a labouring population ready to be exploited under one of the most beautiful skies in the world. It may be so with Egypt some day. Therefore it is ports for exports, and especially military ports, in the Adriatic, the Persian Gulf, on the African coast in Beira, and also in the Pacific, that these schemers of German colonial trade wish to conquer. Their faithful servant, the German Empire, with its armies and ironclads, is at their service for this purpose."

It is this class, then, which by backing both financially and morally the military class has been chiefly responsible for bringing about the war. Not that I mean, in saying so, that the commercial folk of Germany have directly instigated its outbreak at the present moment and in the present circumstances—for many, or most of them, must have seen how dangerous it was likely to prove to their trade. But in respect of the general policy which they have so long pursued they are responsible. One cannot go on for years (and let England, too, remember this) preaching militarism as a means of securing commercial advantage, and then refuse to be answerable for the results to which such a policy may lead. The Junker classes of Prussia and their Kaiser might be suffering from a bad attack of swelled head; vanity and arrogance might be filling them with dreams of world-empire; but there would have been no immediate European war had not the vast trade-interests of Germany come into conflict, or seemed to come into conflict, with the trade-interests of the surrounding nations—had not the financial greed of the nation been stirred, as well as its military vanity.

And talking of general trade and finance, one must not forget to include the enormous powers exercised in the present day by individual corporations and individual financiers who intrude their operations into the sphere of politics. We saw *that* in our own Boer War; and behind the scenes in

Germany to-day similar influences are at work. The Deutsche Bank, with immense properties all over the world, and some £85,000,000 sterling in its hands in deposits alone, initiated financially the Baghdad Railway scheme. Its head, Herr Arthur von Gwinner, the great financier, is a close adviser of the Kaiser. "The railway is already nearly half built, and it represents a German investment of between £16,000,000 and £18,000,000. Let this be thought of when people imagine that Germany and Austria went to war with the idea of avenging the murder of an Archduke. . . . All German trade would suffer if the Baghdad Railway scheme were to fail."[1] Then there is Herr August Thyssen—"King Thyssen"—"who owns coal-mines, rolling mills, harbours, and docks throughout Germany, iron-ore mines in France, warehouses in Russia, and *entrepôts* in nearly every country from Brazil and Argentina to India.[2] He has declared that German interests in Asia Minor must be safeguarded at all costs. But Russia also

[1] See *Nash's Magazine* for October, 1914, article by "Diplomatist."
[2] Ibid.

has large prospective commercial interests in Asia Minor. The moral is clear and needs no enforcing. Such men as these—and many others, the Rathenaus, Siemens, Krupps, Ballins, and Heinekens—exercise in Germany an immense political influence, just as do our financial magnates at home. They represent the peaks and summits of wide-spreading commercial activities whose bases are rooted among the general public. Yet through it all it must not be forgotten that they represent in each case (as I shall explain more clearly presently) the interests of a *class*—the commercial class—but not of the whole nation.

One must, then, modify the first conclusion, that the blame of the war rests with the military class, by adding a second factor, namely, the rise and influence of the commercial class. These two classes, acting and reacting on each other, and pushing—though for different reasons—in the same direction, are answerable, as far as Germany is concerned, for dragging Europe into this trouble; and they must share the blame.

If it is true, as already suggested, that Germany's action has only been that of the spark that fires the magazine, still her part in the affair affords such an extraordinarily illuminating text and illustration that one may be excused for dwelling on it.

Here, in her case, we have the divisions of a nation's life set out in well-marked fashion. We have a military clique headed by a personal and sadly irresponsible ruler; we have a vulgar and much swollen commercial class; and then, besides these two, we have a huge ant's nest of professors and students, a large population of intelligent and well-trained factory workers, and a vast residuum of peasants. Thus we have at least five distinct classes, but of these the last three have—till thirty or forty years ago—paid little or no attention to political matters. The professors and students have had their noses buried in their departmental science and *fach* studies; the artisans have been engrossed with their technical work, and have been only gradually drifting away from their capitalist employers and into the Socialist camp; and the peasants—as elsewhere over the world, absorbed in their laborious and ever-necessary labours—have accepted their fate and paid but little attention to what was going on over their heads. Yet these three last-mentioned classes, forming the great bulk of the nation, have been swept away, and suddenly at the last, into a huge embroilment in which to begin with they had no interest or profit.

This may seem strange, but the process after all is quite simple, and to study it in the case of Germany may throw helpful light on our own affairs. However the blame may be apportioned between the Junker and commercial classes, it is clear that, fired by the Bismarckian programme, and greatly overstretching it, they played into each other's hands. The former relied for the financing of its schemes on the support of the commercials. The latter saw in the militarists a power which might increase Germany's trade-supremacy. Vanity and greed are met together, patriotism and profits have kissed each other. A Navy League and an Army League and an Air League arose. Professors and teachers were subsidized in the universities; the children were taught Pan-Germanism in the schools; a new map of Europe was put before them. An enormous literature grew up on the lines of Treitschke, Houston Chamberlain, and Bernhardi, with novels and romances to illustrate side-issues, and the Press playing martial music. The students and intellectuals began to be infected; the small traders and shopkeepers were moved; and the war-fever gradually spread through the nation. As to the artisans, they may, as I have said, have largely belonged to the Socialist party—with its poll of four million votes in the last election—and in the words of Herr Haase in the Reichstag just before the war, they may have wished to hold themselves apart from "this cursed Imperialist policy"; but when the war actually arrived, and the fever, and the threat of Russia, and the fury of conscription, they perforce had to give way and join in. How on earth could they do otherwise? And the peasants—even if they escaped the fever—could not escape the compulsion of authority nor the old blind tradition of obedience. They do not know, even to-day, why they are fighting; and they hardly know whom they are fighting, but in their ancient resignation they accept the inevitable and shout "Deutschland über Alles" with the rest. And so a whole nation is swept off its feet by a small section of it, and the insolence of a class becomes, as in Louvain and Rheims, the scandal of the world.[1]

And the people bleed; yes, it is always the people who bleed. The trains arrive at the hospital bases, hundreds, positively hundreds of them, full of wounded. Shattered human forms lie in thousands on straw inside the trucks and wagons, or sit painfully reclined in the passenger compartments, their faces grimed, their clothes ragged, their toes protruding from their boots. Some have been stretched on the battlefield for forty-eight hours, or even more, tormented by frost at night, covered with flies by day, without so much as a drink of water. And those that have not already become a mere lifeless heap of rags have been jolted in country carts to some railway-station, and there, or at successive junctions, have been shunted on sidings for endless hours. And now, with their wounds still slowly bleeding or oozing, they are picked out by tender

[1] In order to realize how easy such a process is, we have only to remember the steps by which the outbreak of the Boer War in 1899 was engineered.

hands, and the most crying cases are roughly dressed before consigning to a hospital. And some faces are shattered, hardly recognizable, and some have limbs torn away; and there are internal wounds unspeakable, and countenances deadly pallid, and moanings which cannot be stifled, and silences worse than moans.

Yes, the agony and bloody sweat of battlefields endured for the domination or the ambition of a class is appalling. But in many cases, though more dramatic and appealing to the imagination, one may doubt if it is worse than the year-long and age-long agony of daily life endured for the same reason.

Maeterlinck, in his eloquent and fiery letter to the *Daily Mail* of September 14th, maintained that the whole German nation is equally to blame in this affair—that all classes are equally involved in it, with no *degrees* of guilt. We may excuse the warmth of personal feeling which makes him say this, but we cannot accept the view. We are bound to point out that it is only by some such analysis as the above, and estimation of the method by which the delusions of one class may be communicated to the others, that we can guard ourselves, too, from falling into similar delusions.

I mentioned that besides the growth of the commercial class, a second great cause of the war was the political ignorance of the German people. And this is important. Fifty years ago, and before that, when Germany was divided up into scores of small States and Duchies, the mass of its people had no practical interest in politics. Such politics as existed, as between one Duchy and another, were mere teacup politics. Read Eckermann's *Conversations*, and see how small a part they played in Goethe's mind. That may have been an advantage in one way. The brains of the nation went into science, literature, music. And when, after 1870, the unification of Germany came, and the political leadership passed over to Prussia, the same state of affairs for a long time continued; the professors continued their investigations in the matters of the thyroid gland or the rock inscriptions in the Isle of Thera, but they left the internal regulation of the State and its foreign policy confidently in the hands of the Kaiser and the nominees of the great and rising *bourgeoisie*, and themselves remained unobservant and uninstructed in such matters. It was only when these latter powers declared —as in the Emperor's pan-German proclamation of 1896—that a Teutonic world-empire was about to be formed, and that the study of *welt-politik* was the duty of every serious German, that the thinking and reading portion of the population suddenly turned its attention to this subject. An immense mass of political writings—pamphlets, prophecies, military and economic treatises, romances of German conquest, and the like—naturally many of them of the crudest sort, was poured forth and eagerly accepted by the public, and a veritable Fool's Paradise of German supremacy arose. It is only in this way, by noting the long-preceding ignorance of the German citizen in the matter of politics, his absolute former non-interference in public affairs, and the dazed state of his mind when he suddenly found himself on the supposed pinnacle of world-power—that we can explain his easy acceptance of such cheap and *ad hoc* publications as those of Bernhardi and Houston Chamberlain, and the fact that he was so easily rushed into the false situation of the present war.[1] The absurd *canards* which at an early date gained currency in Berlin—as that the United States had swallowed Canada, that the Afghans in mass were invading India, that Ireland was plunged in civil war—point in the same direction; and so do the barbarities of the Teutonic troops in the matters of humanity and art. For though in all war and in the heat of battle there are barbarities perpetrated, it argues a strange state of the German national psychology that in this case a heartless severity and destruction of the enemy's life and property should have been preached beforehand, and quite deliberately, by professors and militarists, and accepted, apparently, by the general public. It argues, to say the least, a strange want of perception of the very unfavourable impression

[1] Of course we must remember that there has been all along and is now in Germany a very large party, Socialist and other, which has *not* been thus carried away; but for the moment its mouth is closed and it cannot make itself heard.

which such a programme must inevitably excite in the mind of the world at large.

It is, no doubt, pleasant in its way for us British to draw this picture of Germany, and to trace the causes which led the ruling powers there, years ago, to make up their minds for war, because, of course, the process in some degree exonerates us. But, as I have already said, I have dwelt on Germany, not only because she affords such a good illustration of what to avoid, but also because she affords so clear an example of what is going on elsewhere in Europe—in England and France and Italy, and among all the modern nations. We cannot blame Germany without implicitly also blaming these.

What, indeed, shall we say of England? Germany has for years maintained that with her own growing population and her growing trade she needs a more extended seaboard in Europe, and coaling stations and colonies in other regions of the globe, but that England, jealous of commercial supremacy, has been determined to deny her these, and, if possible, to crush her; that she (Germany) has lived in perpetual fear and panic; and that if in this case she has been the first to strike, it has only been because to wait England's opportunity would have been to court defeat. Allowing for the exaggerations inseparable from opposed points of view, is there not some justification for this plea? England, who plunged into the Crimean War in order to *prevent* Russia from obtaining a seaboard and her natural commercial expansion, and who afterwards joined with Russia in order to plunder Persia and to prevent Germany from getting her railways along the Persian Gulf; who calmly appropriated Egypt, with its valuable cotton-lands and market; who, at the behest of a group of capitalists and financiers, turned her great military machine on a little nation of Boer farmers in South Africa; who, it is said,[1] sold 300,000 tons of coal to Russia to aid her fleet against Japan, and at the same time furnished Japan with gold at a high rate of interest for use against Russia —what trust can be placed in her? "England," says Bernhardi, "in spite of all her pretences of a liberal and philan-

[1] See Kropotkin's *War and Capitalism*, p. 12

thropic policy, has never sought any other object than personal advantage and the unscrupulous suppression of her rivals." Let us hope that this "never" is *too* harsh; let us at least say "hardly ever"; but still, are we not compelled to admit that if the rise of commercial ambition in Germany has figured as a danger to *us*, our far greater commercial ambitions have not only figured as a danger to Germany, but, in conjunction with our alliance with France and Russia, her ancient foes, may well have led to a state of positive panic among her people? And if, as the Allies would doubtless say, there was really no need for any such panic, the situation was obviously sufficiently grave to be easily made use of by a military class for its own ends, or by an armaments ring or a clique of financiers for theirs. Indeed, it would be interesting to know what enormous profits Kruppism (to use H. G. Wells' expressive term) *has* already made out of this world-madness. Nor can it be denied that the commercial interest in England, if not deliberately intending to provoke war with Germany, has not been at all sorry to seize this opportunity of laying a rival Power low—if only in order to snatch the said rival's trade. That, indeed, the daily Press reveals only too clearly.

From all this the danger of class-domination emerges more and more into relief. In Prussia the old Feudal caste remains—in a decadent state, certainly, but perhaps for that very reason more arrogant, more vulgar, and less conscious of any *noblesse oblige* than even before. By itself, however, and if unsupported by the commercial class, it would probably have done little harm. In Britain the Feudal caste has ceased to be exclusively military, and has become blended with the commercial class. The British aristocracy now consists largely or chiefly of retired grocers and brewers. Commercialism here has become more confessedly dominant than in Germany, and whereas there the commercial class may *support* the military in its ambitions, here the commercial class *uses* the military as a matter of course and for its own ends. We have become a Nation of Shopkeepers having our own revolvers and machine-guns behind the counter.

And yet not really a Nation of Shopkeepers, but rather a nation ruled by a shop-keeping *class*.

People sometimes talk as if commercial prosperity and the interests of the commercial folk represented the life of the whole nation. That is a way of speaking, and it illustrates certainly a common modern delusion. But it is far from the truth. The trading and capitalist folk are only a class, and they do *not*, properly speaking, represent the nation. They do not represent the land-owning and the farming interests, both of which detest them; they do not represent the artisans and industrial workers, who have expressly formed themselves into unions in order to fight them, and who have only been able to maintain their rights by so doing; they do not represent the labourers and peasants, who are ground under their heel. It would take too long to go into the economics of this subject, interesting though they are.[1] But a very brief survey of facts shows us that wherever the capitalist and trading classes have triumphed —as in England early last century, and until socialistic legislation was called in to check

[1] See note *infra* on "Commercial Prosperity," p. 167.

them—the condition of the mass of the people has by no means improved, rather the contrary. Japan has developed a world trade, and is on the look out for more, yet never before has there been such distress among her mass-populations. Russia has been lately moving in the same direction; her commercial interests are rapidly progressing, but her peasantry is at a standstill, France and Italy have already grown a fat *bourgeoisie*, but their workers remain in a limbo of poverty and strikes. And in all these countries, including Germany, Socialism has arisen as a protest against the commercial order—which fact certainly does not look as if commercialism were a generally acknowledged benefit.

No, commercial prosperity means only the prosperity of a class. Yet such is the curious glamour that surrounds this subject and makes a fetish of statistics about "imports and exports," that nothing is more common than for such prosperity to be taken to mean the prosperity of the nation as a whole. The commercial people, having command of the Press, and of the avenues and highways of public influence, do not find it at all difficult to persuade the nation that *they* are its representatives, and that *their* advantage is the advantage of all. This illusion is only a part, I suppose, of a historical necessity, which as the Feudal regime passes brings into prominence the Commercial regime; but do not let us be deluded by it, nor forget that in submitting to the latter we are being nose-led by a class just as much as the Germans have been in submitting to the Prussian Junkers. Do not let us, at the behest of either class, be so foolish as to set out in vain pursuit of world-empire; and, above all, do not let us, in freeing ourselves from military class-rule, fall under the domination of financiers and commercial diplomats. Let us remember that wars for world-markets are made for the benefit of the merchant *class* and not for the benefit of the mass-people, and that in this respect England has been as much to blame as Germany or any other nation—nay, pretty obviously more so.

What is clearly wanted—and indeed is the next stage of human evolution in England and in all Western lands—is that the people should emancipate themselves from class-domination, class-glamour, and learn to act freely from their own initiative. I know it is difficult. It means a spirit of independence, courage, willingness to make sacrifice. It means education, alertness to guard against the insidious schemes of wire-pullers and pressmen, as well as of militarists and commercials. It means the perception that only through eternal vigilance can freedom be maintained. Yet it is the only true Democracy; and the logic of its arrival is assured to us by the historical necessity that progress in all countries must pass through the preliminary stages of feudalism and commercialism on its way to realize the true life of the mass-peoples.

To-day the uprising of Socialist ideals, of the power of Trade Unions, and especially the formation of International Unions, show us that we are on the verge of this third stage. We are shaping our way towards the real Democracy, with the attainment of which wars—though they will not cease from the world—will certainly become much rarer. The international *entente* already establishing itself among the manual workers of all the European countries—and which has now become an accepted principle of the Labour movement—is a guarantee and a promise of a more peaceful era; and those who know the artisans and peasants of this and other countries know well how little enmity they harbour in their breasts against each other. Racial and religious wars will no doubt for long continue; but wars to satisfy the ambitions of a military clique or a personal ruler, or the ambitions of a commercial group, or the schemes of financiers, or the engineering of the Press—wars from these all too fruitful causes will, under a sensible Democracy, cease. If Britain, during the last twenty years, had really favoured the cause of the People and their international understanding, there would have been no war now, for her espousal of the mass-peoples' cause would have made her so strong that it would have been too risky for any Government to attack her. But of course that could not have happened, for the simple reason that Conservatism and Liberalism are not Democracy. Conservatism is Feudalism, Liberalism is Commercialism, and Socialism only is in its essence Democracy. It is no good scolding at Sir

Edward Grey for making friends with the Russian Government; for his only alternative would have been to join the " International "—which he certainly could not do, being essentially a creature of the commercial regime. The " Balance of Power " and the *ententes* and alliances of Figure-head Governments *had* to go on, till the day—which we hope is at hand—when Figureheads will be no more needed.

IV

THE CASE AGAINST GERMANY

November, 1914.

WITH every wish to do justice to Germany, to whose literature I feel I owe such a debt, and among whose people I have so many personal friends; allowing also the utmost for the general causes in Europe which have been for years leading up towards war—and some of which I have indicated already in the pages above—I still feel it is impossible not to throw on her the *immediate* blame for the present catastrophe.

However we distribute the indictment and the charges among the various parties concerned, whether we accuse mainly the sway of Prussian Militarism or the rise of German Commercialism, or the long tradition and growth of a *Welt-politik* philosophy, or the general political ignorance which gave to these influences such rash and uncritical acceptance; or whether we accuse the somewhat difficult and variable personal equation of the Kaiser himself—the fact still remains that for years and years this war has been by the German Government most deliberately and systematically prepared for. The fact remains that Britain—though for a long period she had foreseen danger and had on the naval side slowly braced herself to meet it—was on the military side caught at the last moment unprepared; that France was so little intending war that a large portion of the nation was actually still protesting against an increase in the size of the standing army; and that Russia—whatever plans she may have had, or not had, in mind—was confessedly at the same period two years or so behind in the organization and completion of her military establishment.

Whether right or wrong, it can hardly be denied that the moment of the precipitation of war was chosen and insisted on by Germany. After Austria's monstrous and insulting dictation to Servia (23rd July), and

Servia's incredibly humble apology (25th), Austria was still not allowed to accept the latter, and the conference proposed (26th July) by Sir E. Grey—though accepted by France, Russia, and Italy—was refused by Germany (27th). On the 28th Austria declared war on Servia. It was perfectly clear to every one that Russia—after what had happened before in 1908-9, with regard to Bosnia and Herzegovina—could not possibly allow this insult to Servia to pass. Germany, therefore, by this move forced Russia's hand; and at a moment when Russia was known or supposed to be comparatively unprepared.[1] France had been involved in some military scandals and was still debating as to the two years' instead of three years' period for her normal military service. The German Ambassador at Vienna had openly said that France was not in a condition for facing a war. England was currently supposed in Germany to be seriously hampered by domestic troubles at home—chiefly of course

[1] It is said that Russia took some steps towards mobilization as early as the 25th. If she did, that would seem quite natural under the circumstances.

among the Irish, but also amongst the Suffragettes (!) *and* by widespread disaffection in India. It was thought, therefore, that England would certainly remain neutral—and I think we may fairly say that the extent to which Germany counted on this expected neutrality is evidenced by her disappointment and public rage when she found that she was mistaken.

Germany's initiative in the matter is further evidenced by her *instant readiness* to attack. She was in Luxemburg within a few hours of the declaration of war with Russia; and it was clearly her intention to "rush" Paris and then turn back upon Russia.

It may be said that from her own point of view Germany was quite right to take the initiative. If she sincerely believed that the *Entente* was plotting her downfall, she was justified in attacking instead of waiting to be attacked. That may be so. It is the line to which General Bernhardi again returns in his latest book (*Britain as Germany's Vassal*, translated by J. Ellis Barker). But it does not alter the fact that this was an immense responsibility to take, and that the immediate onus of the war rests with Germany. If she under all the above circumstances precipitated war, she can hardly be surprised if the judgment of Europe (one may also say the world) is against her. If she has played her cards so badly as to put herself entirely in the wrong, she must naturally "dree her weird."

There remains the case of her treatment of Belgium. Britain certainly—who has only lately assisted at the dismemberment of Persia, and who is even now allowing Russia (in the face of Persian protests) to cross neutral territory in the neighbourhood of Tabriz on her way to attack Turkey, who has uttered, moreover, no word of protest against the late Ukase (of mid-November) by which the independent rights of Finland have been finally crushed—Britain, I say, need talk no cant about Belgian neutrality. Britain, for her own absolute safety, has always required and still requires Belgian neutrality to be respected. And that by itself is a sufficient, and the most honest, reason. But in the eyes of the world at large Germany's deliberate and determined sacrifice of Belgium, simply because the latter stood in the way of the rapid accomplishment of her warlike designs against France (and England), can never be condoned–little Belgium who had never harmed or offended Germany in any way. Add to this her harsh and brutish ill-treatment of the Belgian civilian people, her ravage of their ancient buildings and works of art, and her clearly expressed intention both in word and deed to annex their territory by force should the fortunes of war favour her—all these facts, which we may say are proven beyond the shadow of a doubt, form a most serious indictment. They substantiate the charge that Germany by acting throughout in this high-handed way has deeply violated the natural laws of the Comity of Nations, which are the safeguards of Civilization, and they confirm the rightful claim of Europe to sit in judgment on her.

I say nothing at the moment about the charges of atrocities committed by German troops, partly because such charges are always in warfare made by each side against the other, and partly because their verification should be the subject of a world-inquiry later on. It may be said, however, that the Belgian and French Commissions of inquiry have certainly presented material and evidence which *ought* to be investigated later—material which would hardly be credible of so humane and cultured a people as the Germans, were it not for the fact, alluded to already, of such severities having been deliberately recommended beforehand by the philosophical writers, military and political, who have during the last half-century moulded German public opinion.

England, as I say, is in no position herself to sit in judgment on Germany and lecture her—much as she undoubtedly enjoys doing so. England's long-standing policy of commercial greed, leading to political grab in every part of the world; her infidelity in late years towards small peoples, like the Boers and the Persians; her neglect of treaty obligations and silence about them when they do not suit her; her most dubious alliance with a military despotism like Russia: all render it impossible for her to accuse Germany. The extraordinary thing is that in the face of such prevarications as these, which are patent to the whole world, Britain at any moment of serious crisis always comes forward with the air of utmost sincerity and in an almost saintly pose as the champion of political morality! How is it? The world laughs and talks of *heuchlerei* and *cant Britannique*. But I almost think (perhaps I stretch a point in order to save the credit of my country) that the real cause is not so much British hypocrisy as British *stupidity*—stupidity which keeps our minds in water-tight compartments and prevents us perceiving how confused and inconsistent our own judgments are and how insincere they appear to our neighbours. At any rate, whether the cause is pure hypocrisy or pure stupidity, or whether a Scotch mixture of these, it cannot be denied that its result is most irritating to decent-minded people.

It is curious how a certain strain or vein of temperament, like that just mentioned, will run through a nation's whole life, and colour its actions in all departments, recognized and commented on by the whole outside world, and yet remain unobserved by the nation itself.

Every one who has known the Germans at home—even years back—has been conscious of a certain strain in the Teutonic character which has had a like bearing in the German national life. How shall I describe it? It is a certain want of tact, unperceptiveness—a kind of overbearing simplicity of mind. Whether it be in the train or the hotel or the private house, the German does not always seem to see the personal situation. Whether you prefer to talk or remain silent, whether you wish the window open or shut, whether you desire to partake of such and such a dish or whether you don't—of such little matters he (or she) seems unaware. Perhaps it is that the Teutonic mind is so vigorous that it overrides you without being conscious of doing so, or that it is so convinced of its own rightness; or perhaps it is that the scientific type of mind, depending always on formulæ and statistics, necessarily loses a certain finer quality. Anyhow, the fact remains that sociable, kindly, *gemüthlich* and so forth as the Germans are, there is a lack of delicate touch and perception about them, of gentle manners, and a certain insensitiveness to the opinion of those with whom they have to deal. The strain may not be without its useful bearings in the direction of strength and veracity, but it runs curiously through the national life, and colours deeply, not only the domestic and social relations of the people but their foreign politics also, and even their war tactics and strategy.

I have spoken before of the political ignorance of the German mass-people, which, dating from years back, caused them to be easily led by their empire-building philosophers to a certain very dangerous pinnacle of ambition, and there tempted. The same want of perception of how their actions would be viewed by the world in general caused the Government to act in the most egregiously high-handed manner in the matter of the precipitation and declaration of the war itself, and subsequently likewise in the ruthless invasion of Belgium and treatment of her people and her cities. The want of discernment of what was going on outside the sphere of her own psychology led her into fatal delusions as to the attitude of England, of Ireland, of Belgium, Italy, India, and so forth. It caused her generals to miscalculate and seriously under-estimate the strategic forces opposed to them, both in France and Russia; and in actual battles it has caused them to adopt, with disastrous results, tactics which were foolishly inspired by contempt of the enemy. Without insisting too much on the stories of atrocities—which are still to a certain extent *sub judice*—it does rather appear that even those excesses which the Commissions of inquiry have reported (and which occurred, be it said, chiefly in the early days of the campaign) were due to an intoxication, not merely of champagne but of excited self-glorification and blindness to the human rights of peoples at least as brave as themselves.[1]

However that last point may be, it is certainly curious to think how—whether it be in the case of the German or the English or any other people—a vein of temperament or character may decide a nation's fate or colour its history quite as much as or even more than matters of wealth and armament.

[1] There may possibly be found another explanation of these excesses—namely, in the galling strictness of the Prussian military regime. After years and years of monotonously regulated and official lives, it may be that to both officers and men, in their different ways, orgies of one kind or another came as an almost inevitable reaction.

Personally one feels sorry for the great and admirable German people—though I do not suppose it will matter to them whether one feels sorry or not! And I look forward to the day when there will come a better understanding between them and ourselves—better perhaps than has ever been before—when we shall forgive them their sins against us, and they will forgive us our sins against them, one of which certainly is our meanness and shopkeeperiness in rejoicing in the war as a means of "collaring their trade." I feel sure that the German mass-people will wake up one day to the knowledge that they have been grossly betrayed at home, not only by Prussian militarism but by pan-German commercial philosophy and bunkum, as well as by their own inattention to, and consequent ignorance of, political affairs. And I hope they will wake up to the conviction that Destiny and the gods in this matter are after all bringing them to a conclusion and a consummation far finer than anything they have perhaps imagined for themselves. If, indeed, when the war is over, they are fortunate enough to be compelled by the terms of settlement to abandon their Army and Navy—or all but the merest residue of these—the consequences undoubtedly will be that, freed from the frightful burdens which the upkeep of these entails, they will romp away over the world through an era of unexampled prosperity and influence. Their science, liberated, will give them the lead in many arts and industries; their philosophy and literature, no longer crippled by national vanities, will rise to the splendid world-level of former days; their colonizing enterprise, unhindered by conscriptionist vetoes, will carry them far and wide over the globe; and even their trade will find that without fortified seaports and tariff walls it will, in these days of universal movement and inter-communication, do fully as well as, if not much better than, ever it did before. In that day, however, let us hope that—the more communal conception of public life having prevailed and come to its own—the success of Trade, among any nation or people, will no longer mean the successful manufacture of a dominant and vulgar class, but the real prosperity and welfare of the whole nation, including all classes.

And in that day, possibly, the other nations, witnessing the extraordinary prosperity and success of that one which has abandoned armaments and Kruppisms, will—if they have a grain of sense left in them—follow suit and, voluntarily divesting themselves too of their ancient armour, give up the foolishness of national enmities and jealousies, and adopt the attitude of humanity and peace, which alone can be the worthy and sensible attitude for us little mortals, when we shall have arrived at years of discretion upon the earth.

[Just after writing the above I received the following remarks in a letter of a friend from South America, which may be worth reprinting. He says: "In spite of the events of 1815 and 1870, French 'culture' is supreme to-day over all South America. South America is a suburb of Paris, and French culture has won its triumphs wholly irrespective of the defeat of French arms. Therefore I incline to think that true German culture in science and music will gain rather than lose by the destruction of German arms. Not only will that nation cease to spend its time writing dull military books, but other nations will be more likely to appreciate what there is in German thought and culture when this is no longer offered us at the point of the bayonet! German commerce in South America has suffered rather than gained by talk of 'shining armour.' And the poet, scientist and business man will gain rather than lose if no longer connected with Potsdam."]

V

THE CASE FOR GERMANY

HAVING put in the last chapter some of the points which seem to throw the immediate blame of the war on Germany, it would be only fair in the present chapter to show how in the long run and looking to the general European situation to-day as well as to the history of Germany in the past, the war had become inevitable, and in a sense necessary as a stage in the evolution of European politics.

After the frightful devastation of Germany by the religious dissensions of the early part of the seventeenth century and the Thirty Years War, it fell to Frederick the Great, not only to lay a firm foundation for the Prussian State but to elevate it definitely as a rival to Austria in the leadership of Germany. Thenceforth Prussia grew in power and influence, and became the nucleus of a new Germany. It would almost seem that things could not well have been otherwise. Germany was seeking for a new root from which to grow. Clerical and ultra-Catholic Austria was of no use for this purpose. Bavaria was under the influence of France. Lutheran Prussia attracted the best elements of the Teutonic mind. It seems strange, perhaps, that the sandy wastes of the North-East, and its rather arid, dour population, *should* have become the centre of growth for the new German nation, considering the latter's possession of its own rich and vital characteristics, and its own fertile and beautiful lands; but so it was. Perhaps the general German folk, with their speculative, easygoing, almost sentimental tendencies, *needed* this hard nucleus of Prussianism—and its matter-of-fact, organizing type of ability—to crystallize round.

The Napoleonic wars shattered the old order of society, and spread over Europe the seeds of all sorts of new ideas, in the direction of nationality, republicanism, and so forth. Fichte, stirred by Napoleon's victory at Jena (Fichte's birthplace) and the consequent disaster to his own people, wrote his *Addresses to the German Nation,* pleading eloquently for a "national regeneration." He, like Vom Stein, Treitschke, and many others in their time, came to Berlin and established himself there as in the centre of a new national activity. Vom Stein, about the same time, carried out the magnificent and democratic work by which he established on Napoleonic lines (and much to Napoleon's own chagrin) the outlines of a great and free and federated Germany. Carl von Clausewitz did in the military world much what Stein did in the civil world. He formulated the strategical methods and teachings of Napoleon, and in his book *Vom Krieg* (published 1832) not only outlined a greater military Germany, but laid the basis, it has been said, of all serious study in the art of war. Vom Stein and Clausewitz died in the same year, 1831. In 1834 Heinrich von Treitschke was born.

The three Hohenzollern kings, all named Frederick William, who reigned from the death of Frederick the Great (1786) to the accession of William I (1861) did not count much personally. The first and third of those mentioned were decidedly weak-minded, and the third towards the close of his reign became insane. But the ideas already initiated in Germany continued to expand. The Zollverein was established, the Teutonic Federation became closer, and the lead of Prussia more decided. With the joint efforts of William I and Bismarck the policy became more governmental, more positive, and more deliberate—the policy of consolidation and of aggrandisement; and with this definite programme in view, Bismarck engineered the three wars of 1864, 1866, and 1870, against Denmark, Austria, and France. They all three had the effect of confirming the military power of Prussia. The first war gave her a much desired increase of access to the North Sea; the second led to the treaty with Austria, and ultimately to the formation of the Triple Alliance; the third ended in the definite establishment of the Prussian hegemony, the crowning of William I as Emperor, and the union and consolidation of all the German States under him; but alas! it left a seed of evil in the wresting of Alsace-Lorraine from France. For France never forgave this. Bismarck and Moltke knew she would not forgive, and were sorely tempted to engineer a *second* war which should utterly disable her; but this war never came off. The seed of Revenge, however, remained with France, and the seed of Fear with Germany; and these two things were destined to lead to a harvest of disaster.

In 1866 Treitschke came to Berlin. Though Saxon by birth, he became ultra-Prussian in sympathy and temperament. Somewhat deaf, and by no means yielding or facile in temper, he was not cut out for a political career. But politics were his interest; his lectures on history were successful at Leipzig and had still more scope at Berlin. He became the strongest of German Unionists, and with a keen but somewhat narrow mind took an absolute pleasure in attacking every movement or body of people that seemed to him in any way to stand in the path of Germany's advancement, or not to assist in her consolidation. Thus he poured out his wrath in turn on Saxony (his own land) and on Hanover, on the Poles, the Socialists, and the

Catholics, and ultimately in his later years on Britain.[1]

He conceived, following the lines of the Prussian tradition, that Germany had a great military mission to fulfil. Her immense energy and power, which had bulked so large in the early history of Europe, and which had been so sadly scattered during the religious wars, was now to come to its own again. She was to make for herself a great place in Europe, and to expand in colonies over the world. It was a pleasing and natural ambition, and the expression of it gave a great vogue and popularity to Treitschke's lectures. The idea was enormously reinforced by the cause which I have already mentioned and dwelt upon—the growth of the commercial interest in Germany. From 1870 onwards this growth was huge and phenomenal. In a comparatively short time a whole new social class sprang up in the land, and a whole new public

[1] "A German," he said, "could not live long in the atmosphere of England—an atmosphere of sham, prudery, conventionality, and hollowness"! See article on "Treitschke," by W. H. Dawson, in the *Nineteenth Century* for January 1915.

opinion. If expansion from the point of view of Junker ambition had been desirable before, the same from the point of view of the financial and trading classes was doubly so now. If a military irruption into the politics of the world was favoured before, it was clamoured for now when a powerful class had arisen which not only called the tune but could pay the piper.

Thus by the combination of military and commercial interests and entanglements the web of Destiny was woven and Germany was hurried along a path which–though no definite war was yet in sight—was certain to lead to war. The general military programme of Treitschke, the conviction that force and force alone could give his country her rightful place in the world, was more and more cordially adopted. In a sense this was a perfectly natural and logical programme, and amid the surrounding European conditions excusable—as I shall point out presently. But before long it became a weird enthusiasm, almost an obsession. It was taken up over the land, and repeated in a thousand books and on as many platforms. One of these propagandists was

General von Bernhardi, who entered in more detail into the technical and strategical aspects of the programme. The rude and almost brutal frankness of both writers may be admired; but the want of real depth and breadth of view cannot be concealed and must be deplored. The arguments in favour of force, of unscrupulousness, of terrorism are—especially in Bernhardi[1]—casuistical to a degree. They are those of a man who is determined to press his country into war at all costs, and who will use any kind of logic as long as it will lead in his direction. The whole movement—largely made possible by the political ignorance of the mass-people, of which I have spoken in a former chapter—culminated in an extraordinary national fever of ambition; and in the announcement of schemes for the Germanization of the world, almost juvenile in the want of experience and the sense of proportion which they display. It would not be fair to take one writer as conclusive; but as a *specimen* of the kind of thing we may quote the following extract (given by Mr. H. A. L.

[1] The influence, however, of Bernhardi in his own country has been somewhat exaggerated in England.

Fisher, the Oxford historian, in his able brochure *The War: Its Causes and Issues*) from the writings of Bronsart von Schellendorf: "Do not let us forget the civilizing task which the decrees of Providence have assigned to us. Just as Prussia was destined to be the nucleus of Germany, so the regenerated Germany shall be the nucleus of a future Empire of the West. And in order that no one shall be left in doubt, we proclaim from henceforth that our continental nation has a right to the sea, not only to the North Sea, but to the Mediterranean and Atlantic. Hence we intend to absorb one after another all the provinces which neighbour on Prussia. We will successively annex Denmark, Holland, Belgium, Northern Switzerland, then Trieste and Venice, finally Northern France from the Sambre to the Loire. This programme we fearlessly pronounce. It is not the work of a madman. The Empire we intend to found will be no Utopia. We have ready to our hands the means of founding it, and no coalition in the world can stop us."

Bronsart von Schellendorf (1832-91) was one of the Prussian Generals who negotiated the surrender of the French at Sedan. He became Chief of the Staff, and War Minister (1883-9), and wrote on Tactics, etc. His above utterance, therefore, cannot be neglected as that of an irresponsible person.

There is, as I have already had occasion to say, a certain easygoing absurdity in the habit we commonly have of talking of nations—"Germany," "France," "England," and so forth—as if they were simple and plainly responsible persons or individuals, when all the time we know perfectly well that they are more like huge whirlpools of humanity caused by the impact and collision of countless and often opposing currents flowing together from various directions. Yet there is this point of incontestable similarity between nations and individual persons, that both occasionally go mad! If Germany was afflicted by a kind of madness or divine *dementia* previous to the present war, Britain can by no means throw that in her teeth, for Britain certainly went mad over Mafeking; and it was sheer madness that in 1870 threw the people of France and Napoleon III—utterly unready for war as they were, and over a most trifling quarrel—into the arms of Bismarck for the fulfilment of his schemes.

But that some sort of madness did, in consequence of the above-mentioned circumstances, seize the German people shortly before the outbreak of the present war we can hardly doubt, though (remembering the proverb) we must not put the blame for that on her, but on the gods. It was a heady intoxication, caused largely, I believe, by that era of unexampled commercial prosperity following upon a period of great political and military expansion, and confirmed by the direct incitement of the military and political teachers I have mentioned. All these things, acting on a people unskilled in politics—of whom Bernhardi himself says "We are a non-political people"[1]—had their natural effect. But it seems part of the irony of fate that at this very juncture Germany should have fallen under the influence of a man who of all the world was perhaps least fitted to guide her steadily

[1] It seems that the same remark is made about the Germans in the U.S.A., that they take little interest in politics there.

through a difficult crisis. "We all know the Kaiser," says Mr. Fisher, "the most amazing and amusing figure on the great stage of politics. The outlines of his character are familiar to everybody, for his whole life is spent in the full glare of publicity. We know his impulsiveness, his naiveté, his heady fits of wild passion, his spacious curiosity and quick grasp of detail, his portentous lack of humour and delicacy, his childish vanity and domineering will. A character so romantic, spontaneous, and robust must always be a favourite with the British people, who, were his lunacies less formidable, would regard him as the most delectable burlesque of the age."

However the British generally may regard him, it is certain that the German nation accepted him as their acclaimed leader. Clever, good-looking, versatile, imperious, fond of the romantic pose, Wilhelm was exactly the hero in shining armour that would capture the enthusiasm of this innocent people. They idolized him. And it is possible that their quick response confirmed him in his rather generous estimate of his own capabilities. He dismissed Bismarck and became his own Foreign Secretary, and entered upon a perilous career as Imperial politician, under the ægis of God and the great tradition of the Hohenzollerns, a career made all the more perilous by his constant change of rôle and his real uncertainty as to his own mind. His "seven thousand speeches and three hundred uniforms" were only the numerous and really emblematic disguises of a character unable to concentrate persistently and effectively on any one settled object. With a kind of theatrical sincerity he made successive public appearances as War Lord or William the Peaceful, as Artist, Poet, Architect, Biblical Critic, Preacher, Commercial Magnate, Generalissimo of land forces and Creator of a World Navy; and with Whitman he might well have said, "I can resist anything better than my own diversity."

If Wilhelm II was popular (as he was) among his own mass-people, it may well be guessed that he was a perfect terror to his own political advisers and generals. Undoubtedly a large share of responsibility for the failure of German diplomacy before the war, and of German strategy during the war, must be laid to the account of his ever-changing plans and ill-judged interferences. It is difficult, indeed, to imagine a character more dangerous as a great nation's leader. But out of dangers great things do often arise. A kind of fatality, as I have said, has enveloped the whole situation, and still leads on to new and pregnant evolutions for the German people and for the whole world. Germany will in the end be justified, but in a way far different from what she imagined.

Up to the period of Germany's rising commercial prosperity Germany and England had been on fairly friendly terms. There was no particular cause of difference between them. But when Commercial and Colonial expansion became a definite and avowed object of the former's policy, she found, whereso she might look, that Britain was there, in the way—" everywhere British colonies, British coaling stations, and floating over a fifth of the globe the British flag." Could anything be more exasperating? And these " absent-minded beggars " the

English, without any forethought or science or design, without Prussian organization or Prussian bureaucracy and statecraft, had simply walked into this huge inheritance without knowing what they were doing! It certainly was most provoking. But what England had done why should not Germany do—and do it indeed much better, with due science and method? Britain had shown no scruple in appropriating a fifth part of the globe, and dealing summarily with her opponents, whether savage or civilized; why should Germany show scruple?

And it must be confessed that here Germany had a very good case. Imitation is the sincerest form of flattery. And if Germany, approving Britain's example, could only show herself strong enough to imitate it in actual fact, Britain at least could not blame her. Besides, in her internal industrial development Germany was already showing her equality with England. In her iron and steel manufactures, her agricultural machines, her cutlery, her armament works, her glass works, her aniline dyes, her toys, and her production of a thousand and one articles (like lamps) of household use, she was showing a splendid record—better in some ways than England. For while England was losing ground, Germany was gaining all the time. England was becoming degenerate and lacking in enterprise. The Zeiss glassworks at Jena have now become the centre of the optical-glass industry of the world. Carl Zeiss, the founder, tried hard at one time to get the English glass-makers to turn out a special glass for his purpose, with very high refractive index. They would not trouble about it. Zeiss consequently was forced to take the matter up himself, succeeded at last in getting such glass made in Germany, and " collared " the trade. The same happened in other departments.

A certain amount of friction arose. The Germans at one time, knowing the English reputation for cutlery, marked their knives and razors as " made in Scheffield." The English retaliated in what seemed an insulting way, by marking the Fatherland's goods as " made in Germany." With Germany's success, commercial jealousy between the two nations (founded on the utterly mistaken but popular notion that the financial prosperity of the country you trade with is inimical to your own prosperity) began to increase. On the German side it was somewhat bitter. On the English side, though not so bitter, it was aggravated by the really shameful ignorance prevailing in this country with regard to things German, and the almost entire neglect of the German tongue in our schools and universities and among our literary folk. As an expression (though one hopes exceptional) of commercial jealousy on our side I may quote a passage from a letter from a business friend of mine in Lancashire. He says: "I remember about a *fortnight before* the war broke out with Germany having a conversation with a business man in Manchester, and he said to me that we most certainly ought to join in with the other nations and sweep the Germans off the face of the earth; I asked him *why*, and his only answer was, '*Look at the figures of Germany's exports; they are almost as high as ours!*' All he had against them was their enterprise—commercial jealousy."

On the other hand, the head of a large warehouse told me only a few days later that when travelling in Germany for his firm some fifteen years ago he had a conversation with a German, in the course of which he (the Englishman) said: "I find your people so obliging and friendly that I think surely whatever little differences there are between us as nations will be dispelled by closer intercourse, and so all danger of war will pass away." "No," replied the German, "you are quite mistaken. You and I are friendly; but that is only as individuals. As nations we shall never rest till we have war. The English nation may well be contented because they have already *got* all the good things of the Earth—their trade, their ports, their colonies; but Germany will not allow this to go on for ever. She will fight for her rightful position in the world; she will challenge England's mercantile supremacy. She will have to do so, and she will not fail."[1]

Thus the plot thickened; the entanglement increased. The Boer War roused ill-feeling between England and Germany. The German Navy Bill followed in 1900, and the Kaiser announced his intention of

[1] This attitude is exactly corroborated by Herr Maximilian Harden's manifesto, originally published in *Die Zukunft*, and lately reprinted in the *New York Times*.

creating a sea-power the equal of any in the world. Britain of course replied with her Navy Bills; and the two countries were committed to a mad race of armaments. The whole of Europe stood by anxious. Fear and Greed, the two meanest of human passions, ruled everywhere. Fear of a militarist Germany began to loom large upon the more pacific States of Europe. On the other hand, the fatality of Alsace-Lorraine loomed in Germany, full of forebodings of revenge. France had found a friend in Russia—a sinister alliance. Britain, convinced that trouble was at hand, came to an understanding with France in 1904 and with Russia in 1907. The Triple Entente was born as a set-off against the Triple Alliance. The Agadir incident in 1911 betrayed the purely commercial nature of the designs of the four Powers concerned —France, Spain, England, and Germany— and a war over the corpse of Morocco was only narrowly avoided. Germany felt quite naturally that she was the victim of a plot, and thenceforth was alternately convulsed by mad Ambition and haunted by a lurking Terror.

And now we come to the last act of the great drama. So far the relations of Germany with Russia had not been strained. If there was any fear of Russia, it was quite in the background. The Junkers—themselves half Slavs—had supplied a large number of the Russian officials, men like Plehve and Klingenberg; the Russian bureaucracy was founded on and followed the methods of the German. The Japanese War called Russia's attention away to another part of the world, and at the same time exposed her weakness. But if Germany was not troubled about Russia, a different sentiment was growing up in Russia itself. The people there were beginning to hate the official German influence and its hard atmosphere of militarism, so foreign to the Russian mind. They were looking more and more to France. Bismarck had made a great mistake in the Treaty of Berlin—a mistake which he afterwards fully recognized and regretted. He had used the treaty to damage and weaken Russia, and had so thrown Russia into the arms of France.

A strange Nemesis was preparing. The

programme of German expansion—natural enough in itself, but engineered by Prussia during all this long period with that kind of blind haughtiness and overbearing assurance which indeed is a "tempting of Providence"—had so far not concerned itself much about Muscovite policy; but now there arose a sudden fear of danger in that quarter. Hitherto the main German "objective" had undoubtedly been England and France, Belgium and Holland—the westward movement towards the Atlantic and the great world. But now all unexpectedly, or at any rate with dramatic swiftness, Russia appeared on the scenes, and there was a *volte face* towards the East. The Balkan Wars of 1912 and 1913 broke out. Whatever simmerings of hostility there may have been between Germany and Russia before, the relations of the two now became seriously strained. The Balkan League, formed under Russian influence, was nominally directed against Turkey; but it was also a threat to Austria. It provided a powerful backing to the Servian agitation, it was a step towards the dissolution of Austria, and it decisively closed the door on Germany's ambition to reach Salonika and to obtain a direct connection with the Baghdad Railway. Germany and Austria all at once found themselves isolated in the midst of Europe, with Russia, Servia, France, and England hostile on every side. It was indeed a tragic situation, and all the more so when viewed as the sorry outcome and culmination of a hundred years of Prussian diplomacy and statecraft.

Why under these circumstances Austria (with Germany of course behind her) should have dictated most insulting terms to Servia, and then refused to accept Servia's most humble apology, is difficult to understand. The only natural explanation is that the Germanic Powers on the whole thought it best, even as matters stood, to precipitate war; that notwithstanding all the complications, they thought that the long-prepared-for hour had come. The German White Book puts the matter as a mere *necessity* of self-defence. "Had the Servians been allowed, with the help of Russia and France, to endanger the integrity of the neighbouring Monarchy much longer, the consequence must have been the gradual disruption of Austria and the subjection of the whole Slav world to the Russian sceptre, with the result that the position of the German race in Central Europe would have become untenable"; but it is obvious that this plea is itself untenable, since it makes a quite distant and problematic danger the excuse for a sudden and insulting blow—for a blow, in fact, almost certain to precipitate the danger!

How the matter was decided in Berlin we cannot at present tell, or what the motives exactly were. It seems rather probable that the Kaiser threw his weight on the side of peace. The German Executive at any rate saw that the great war they had so long contemplated and so long prepared for was close upon them—only in an unexpected form, hugely complicated and threatening. They must have realized the great danger of the situation, but they very likely may have thought that by another piece of bluff similar to that of 1908-9 they might intimidate Russia a second time; and they believed that Russia was behindhand in her military preparations. They also, it appears, thought that England would not fight, being too much preoccupied with Ireland, India, and other troubles. And so it may have seemed that Now was the psychological moment.

Austria opened with war on Servia (28th of July), and the next day Russia declared a considerable though not complete mobilization. From that moment a general conflagration was practically inevitable. The news of Russia's warlike movement caused a perfect panic in Berlin. The tension of feeling swung round completely for the time being from enmity against England and France to fear of Russia. The final mobilization of the Russian troops (31st of July) was followed by the telegrams between the Kaiser and the Tsar, and by the formal mobilization (really already complete) of the German Army and Navy on the 1st of August. War was declared at Berlin on the 1st of August, and the same or next day the German forces entered Luxemburg. On August 4th they entered Belgium, and war was declared by England against Germany.

Looking back at the history of the whole affair, one seems to see, as I have said, a kind of fatality about it. The great power and vigour of the German peoples, shown by their early history in Europe, had been broken up by the religious and other dissensions of the sixteenth and seventeenth centuries. It fell to Prussia to become the centre of organization for a new Germany. The rich human and social material of the German States—their literary, artistic, and scientific culture, their philosophy, their learning—clustered curiously enough round the hard and military nucleus of the North. It was perhaps their instinct and, for the time, their salvation to do so. The new Germany, hemmed in on all sides by foreign Powers, could only see her way to reasonable expansion and recognition, and a field for her latent activities, by the use of force, military force. A long succession of political philosophers drilled this into her. She embarked in small wars and always with success. She became a political unity and a Great Power in Europe. And then came her commercial triumph. Riches beyond all expectation flowed in; and a mercantile class arose in her midst whose ideals of life were of a corresponding character—the ideals of the wealthy shopkeeper. What wonder that, feeling her power, feeling herself more than ever baulked of her rights, she cast her eyes abroad, and coveted the imperial and commercial supremacy of the world?

In this she had the example of Britain before her. Britain had laid land to land and market to market over the globe, and showed no particular scruple in the matter. Why should not Germany do the same? It was true that Britain always carried the Bible with her—but this was mere British cant. Britain carried the Bible in her left hand, but in her right a sword; and when she used the latter she always let the former drop. Germany could do likewise—but without that odious pretence of morality, and those crocodile tears over the unfortunates whom she devoured. It was only a question of Might and Organization and Armament.

So far Germany seems to have had a perfectly good case; and though we in England might not like her ambitions, we could not reasonably find fault with motives so perfectly similar to our own. We might, indeed, make a grievance of the frank brutality displayed in her methods and the defence of them; but then, she might with equal right object to our everlasting pretence of "morality," and our concealment of mercenary and imperial aims under the cloak of virtue and innocence. One really must confess that it is difficult to say which is the worse.

But if the crystallization of Germany round the Prussian nucleus was for the time the source of Germany's success, it is a question whether it is not even now becoming something quite different, and the likely cause of a serious downfall. It would seem hardly probable that the amalgamation between elements so utterly dissimilar can permanently endure. The kindly, studious, sociable, rather naïvely innocent German mass-people dragged by the scruff of the neck into the arena of militarism and world-politics, may for a time have had their heads turned by the exalted position in which they found themselves; but it is not likely that they will continue for long to enjoy the situation. With no great instinct for politics, nor any marked gift of tact and discernment, unsuccessful as a rule as colonists,[1] and

[1] Though this is only, perhaps, true of their State colonies. In their individual and missionary colonizing groups, and as pioneer settlers, they seem to have succeeded well.

with no understanding of how to govern —except on the Prussian lines, which are every day becoming more obsolete and less adapted to the modern world—the rôle which their empire-building philosophers set out for them is one which they are eminently unfitted to fulfil. It is sad, but we cannot blame them for the defect. They blame the world in general for siding against them in this affair, but do not see that in most cases it has been their own want of perception which has left them on the wrong side of the hedge.

Bismarck, with his " Blood and Iron " policy, made a huge blunder in not perceiving that in the modern world spiritual forces are arising which must for ever discredit the same. He emphasized the blunder by wresting Alsace-Lorraine from France, and again by crippling Russia in the treaty of 1878—thus making enemies where generosity might have brought him friends. The German Executive in July of last year (1914) showed extraordinary want of tact in not seeing that Russia, rebuffed in 1908 over Bosnia and Herzegovina, would never put up with a *second* insult of the same kind over Servia. The same Government was strangely unable to perceive that whatever it might tactically gain by the invasion and devastation of Belgium would be more than lost by the moral effect of such action on the whole world; and notwithstanding its army of spies, it had not the sense to see that England, whether morally bound to or not, was certain, at all costs, to fight in defence of Belgium's neutrality. So true it is that without the understanding which comes from the heart, all the paraphernalia of science and learning and the material results of organization and discipline are of little good.

But however we choose to apportion the blame or at least the responsibility for the situation among the various Governments concerned, the main point and the main lesson of it all is to see that any such apportionment does not much matter! As long as our Governments are constructed as they are—that is, on the principle of representing, not the real masses of their respective peoples, but the interests of certain classes, especially the commercial, financial, and military classes—so long will such wars be inevitable. The real blame rests, not with the particular Foreign policy of this or that country but with the fact that Europe, already rising through her mass-peoples into a far finer and more human and spiritual life than of old, still lies bound in the chains of an almost Feudal social order.

When the great German mass-peoples find this out, when they discover the little rift in the lute which now separates their real quality from the false standards of their own dominant military and commercial folk, then their true rôle in the world will begin, and a glorious rôle it will be.

VI

THE HEALING OF NATIONS[1]

IT is quite possible that the little rift within the lute, alluded to in the concluding paragraph of last chapter, may widen so far as to cause before long great internal changes and reconstructions in Germany herself; but short of that happening, it would seem that there is no alternative for the Allies but to continue the war until her Militarism can be put out of court, and that for long years to come. There is no alternative, because she has revealed her hand too clearly as a menace—if she should prevail—of barbarous force to the whole world. It is this menace which has roused practically the whole world against her. And there is this amount of good in the situation, namely, that while

[1] Reprinted by permission from the *English Review* for January, 1915.

with the victory of Germany a German "terror" might be established through the world, with the victory of the Allies neither England, nor France, nor Russia, nor little Belgium, nor any other country, could claim a final credit and supremacy. With the latter victory we shall be freed from the nightmare claim of any one nation's world-empire.

But in order to substantiate this result England must also abdicate her claim. She must abdicate her mere crass insistence on commercial supremacy. The "Nation of Shopkeepers" theory, which has in the past made her the hated of other nations, which has created within her borders a vulgar and unpleasant class—the repository of much arrogant wealth—must cease to be the standard of her life. I have before me at this moment a manifesto of "The British Empire League," patronized by royalty and the dukes, and of which Lord Rothschild is treasurer. The constitution of the League was framed in 1895; and I note with regret that positively the five "principal objects of the League" mentioned therein have solely to do with the extension and facilitation of Britain's trade, and the "co-operation of the military and naval forces of the Empire with a special view to the due protection of the trade routes." Not a word is said *in the whole manifesto* about the human and social responsibilities of this vast Empire; not a word about the guardianship and nurture of native races, their guidance and assistance among the pitfalls of civilization; not a word about the principles of honour and just dealing with regard to our civilized neighbour-nations in Europe and elsewhere; not a word about the political freedom and welfare of all classes at home. One rubs one's eyes, and looks at the document again; but it is so. Its one inspiration is—Trade. Seeing that, I confess to a sinking of the heart. Can we blame Germany for struggling at all costs to enlarge her borders, when *that* is what the British Empire means?

Until we rise, as a nation, to a conception of what we mean by our national life, finer and grander than a mere counting of trade-returns, what can we expect save failure and ill-success?

Possibly in the conviction that she is fighting for a worthy object (the ending of militarism), and in the determination (if sincerely carried out) of once more playing her part in the world as the protector of small nations, Britain may find her salvation, and a cause which will save her soul. It is certainly encouraging to find that there is a growing feeling in favour of the recognition and rehabilitation of the small peoples of the world. If it is true that Britain by her grasping Imperial Commercialism in the past (and let us hope that period *is* past) has roused jealousy and hatred among the other nations, equally is it true that Germany to-day, by her dreams of world-conquest, has been rousing hatred and fear. But the day has gone by of world-empires founded on the lust of conquest, whether that conquest be military or commercial. The modern peoples surely are growing out of dreams so childish as that. The world-empire of Goethe and Beethoven is even now far more extensive, far more powerful, than that which Wilhelm II and his Junkers are seeking to encompass. There is something common, unworthy, in the effort of domination; and while the Great Powers have thus vulgarized themselves, it is the little countries who have gone forward in the path of progress. "In modern Europe what do we not owe to little Switzerland, lighting the torch of freedom six hundred years ago, and keeping it alight through all the centuries when despotic monarchies held the rest of the European Continent? And what to free Holland, with her great men of learning and her painters surpassing those of all other countries save Italy? So the small Scandinavian nations have given to the world famous men of science, from Linnæus downwards, poets like Tegner and Björnson, scholars like Madvig, dauntless explorers like Fridthiof Nansen. England had, in the age of Shakespeare, Bacon, and Milton, a population little larger than that of Bulgaria to-day. The United States, in the days of Washington and Franklin and Jefferson and Hamilton and Marshall, counted fewer inhabitants than Denmark or Greece."[1]

In all their internal politics and social advancement, Switzerland, Holland, Denmark, Norway and Sweden, Finland (until the paw of the Bear was on her) and Bel-

[1] Lord Bryce in the *Daily Chronicle*, October, 1914.

gium (till the claw of the Spread-Eagle) have been well to the fore. It is they who have carried on the banner of idealism which Germany herself uplifted when she was a small people or a group of small peoples. It is they who have really had prosperous, healthy, independent, and alert populations. How much more interesting, we may say, would Europe be under the variety of such a regime than under the monotonous bureaucracy and officialism of any Great Power! And to some such scheme we must adhere. It would mean, of course, the alliance of all the States of Western Europe, large and small (and including both a remodelled Germany and a largely remodelled Austria) in one great Federation—whose purpose would be partly to unite and preserve Europe against any common foe, from the East or elsewhere, and partly to regulate any overweening ambition of a member of the Federation, such as might easily become a menace to the other members. A secondary but most important result of the formation of such a United States of Europe would be that while each State would probably preserve a small military establishment of its own, the enormous and fatal incubus of the present armaments system would be rendered unnecessary, and so at last the threat of national bankruptcy and ruin, which has of late pursued the nations like an evil dream, might pass away. [But in that matter of finance it cannot be disguised that a terrible period still awaits the European peoples. Already the moneylenders sitting on their chests form a veritable nightmare; but with fresh debts by the thousand million sterling being contracted, there is great danger that the mass-peoples beneath will be worse paralysed and broken even than they are now—unless, indeed, with a great effort they rouse themselves and throw off the evil burden.]

That the world is waking up to a recognition of *racial* rights—that is, the right of each race to have as far as possible its own Government, instead of being lorded over by an alien race—is a good sign; and a European settlement along that line must be pressed for. At last, after centuries of discomfort, we at home are finding our solution of the Irish question in this very obvious way; and it may be that Europe, tired of war, may finally have the sense to adopt the same principle. Of course, there are cases where populations are so mixed, as, for instance, the Czechs and Slovaks and Germans in Bohemia and Moravia, or where small colonies of one race are so embedded in the midst of another race, as are the Germans among the Roumanians of Transylvania, that this solution may be difficult. That is no reason, however, why the general principle should not be applied. It *must*, indeed, be applied if Europe is not to return to barbarism.

And it interests us—having regard to what I have said about *class* rule being so fruitful a cause of war—to remember that the rule of one race by another always does mean class rule. The alien conquerors who descend upon a country become the military and landlord caste there. Thus the Norman barons in England, the English squires in Ireland, the Magyars in Hungary, the German barons in East Prussia and the Baltic provinces, and so forth. They make their profit and maintain themselves out of the labour and the taxation of the subject peoples.

In the earlier forms of social life, when men lived in tribes, a rude equality and democracy prevailed; there was nothing that could well be called class-government; there was simply custom and the leadership of the elders of the tribe. Then with the oncoming of what we call civilization, and the growth of the sense of property, differences arose–accumulations of wealth and power by individuals, enslavements of tribes by other tribes; and classes sprang up, and class-government, and so the material of endless suffering and oppression and hatred and warfare. I have already explained (in the Introduction) that Class in itself as the mere formation within a nation of groups of similar occupation and activity–working harmoniously with each other and with the nation–is a perfectly natural and healthy phenomenon; it is only when it means groups pursuing their own interests counter to each other and to the nation that it becomes diseased. There will come a time when the class-element in this latter sense will be ejected from society, and society will return again to its democratic form and structure. There will be no want, in that time, of variety of occupation and talent, or of differentiation in the social organism; quite the contrary; but simply there will be no predatory or parasitical groups within such organism, whose interests will run counter to the whole, and which will act (as such classes act now) as foci and seed-beds of disease and strife within the whole. With a return to the recognition of racial rights and autonomies over the world, it is clear that one great cause of strife will be removed, and we shall be one step nearer to the ending of the preposterous absurdity of war.

And talking about the difficulty of sorting out mixed populations, or of dealing with small colonies of one race embedded in the midst of another race, it is evident that once you get rid of autocratic or military or class-government of any kind, and return to democratic forms, this difficulty will be much reduced or disappear. Small democratic communes are perfectly simple to form in groups of any magnitude or minuteness which may be desirable; and such groups would easily federate or ally themselves with surrounding democracies of alien race, whereas if lorded over by alien conquerors they would be in a state of chronic rebellion. Of such democratic alliance and federation of peoples of totally different race, Switzerland supplies a well-recognized and far-acclaimed example.

That in the future there will be an outcry in favour of Conscription made by certain parties in Britain goes without saying; but that must be persistently opposed. The nation says it is fighting to put down Militarism. Why, then, make compulsory militarism foundational in our national life? To abolish militarism *by* militarism is like "putting down Drink" by swallowing it! The whole lesson of this war is against conscription. Germany could never have "imposed herself" on Europe without it. And yet her soldiers, brave as they naturally are, and skilfully as they have fought, have not done themselves justice. How could they under such conditions—forced into battle by their officers, flung in heaps on the enemy's guns? The voluntary response in Britain to the call to arms has been inspiriting; and if voluntaryism means momentary delay in a crisis, still it means success in the end. No troops have fought more finely than the British. Said Surgeon-General Evatt, speaking in London in October—and General Evatt's word in such a matter ought to carry weight: "After long experience in studying Russian, German, Bavarian, Saxon, French, Spanish, and American fighting units, my verdict is unhesitatingly in favour of the British. . . . What has occurred lately has been a splendid triumph of citizenship, because people were allowed their proper liberty and the consciousness of freely sharing in a great Empire."

Besides it must always be remembered that conscription gives a Government power to initiate an iniquitous war, whereas voluntaryism keeps the national life clean and healthy. A free people will not fight for the trumped-up schemes and selfish machinations of a class—not, indeed, unless they are grossly deceived by Press and Class plots. Anyhow, to force men to fight in causes which they do not approve, to compel them to adopt a military career when their temperaments are utterly unsuited to such a thing, or when their consciences or their religion forbid them—these things are both foolish and wicked.

If the nation wants soldiers it must pay for them. England, for example, is rolling in wealth; and it is simply a scandal that the wealthy classes should sit at home in comfort and security and pay to the man in the trenches—who is risking his life at every moment, and often living in such exhaustion and misery as actually to wish for the bullet which will *end* his life—no more than the minimum wage of an ordinary day-labourer; and that they should begrudge every penny paid to his dependents—whether he be living or dead—or to himself when he returns, a lifelong cripple, to his home. To starve and stint your own soldiers, to discourage recruiting, and then to make the consequent failure of men to come forward into an excuse for conscription is the meanest of policies. As a matter of fact, the circumstances of the present war show that with anything like decent reward for their services there is an abundant, an almost over-abundant, supply of men ready to flock to the standard of their country in a time of necessity. Nor must it be forgotten, in this matter of pay, that the general type and average of our forces to-day, whether naval or military, is far higher than it was fifty years ago. The men are just as plucky, and more educated, more alert, more competent in every way. To keep them up to this high standard of efficiency they need a high standard of care and consideration.

It may, however, be said—in view of our present industrial conditions, and the low standard of physical health and vitality prevailing among the young folk of our large towns—that physical drill and scout training, including ambulance and other work, and qualification in *some* useful trade, might very well be made a part of our general educational system, for rich and poor alike, say between the ages of sixteen and eighteen. Such a training would to each individual boy be immensely valuable, and by providing some rudimentary understanding of military affairs and the duties of public service and citizenship, would enable him to choose *how* he could be helpful to the nation—provided always he were not forced to make his choice in a direction distasteful or repugnant to him. In any good cause, as in a war of *defence* against a foreign enemy, it is obvious enough, as I have said, that there would be plenty of native enthusiasm forthcoming without legal or official pressure. However, I have enlarged a little on the subject of Conscription in a later chapter, and will say no more here.

But the burning and pressing question is: Why should we—we, the "enlightened and civilized" nations of Europe—get involved in these senseless wars at all? And surely *this* war will, of all wars, force an answer to the question. Here, for the last twenty years, have these so-called Great Powers been standing round, all professing that their one desire is peace, and all meanwhile arming to the teeth; each accusing the others of militant intentions, and all lamenting that "war is inevitable." Here they have been forming their *Ententes* and Alliances, carrying on their diplomatic cabals and intrigues, studying the map and adjusting the Balance of Power—all, of course, with the best intentions—and lo! with the present result! What nonsense! What humbug! What an utter bankruptcy of so-called diplomacy! When will the peoples themselves arise and put a stop to this fooling—the people who give their lives and pay the cost of it all? If the present-day diplomats and Foreign Ministers have sincerely striven for peace, then their utter incapacity and futility have been proved to the hilt, and they must be swept away. If they have not sincerely striven for peace, but only pretended to so strive, then also they must be swept away, for deceit in such a matter is unpardonable.

And no doubt the latter alternative is the true one. There has been a pretence of the Governments all round—a pretence of deep concern for humanity and the welfare of the mass-peoples committed to their charge; but the real moving power beneath has been *class*-interest—the interest of the great commercial class in each nation, with its acolyte and attendant, the military or aristocratic. It is this class, with its greeds and vanities and suspicions and jealousies, which is the cause of strife; the working-masses of the various nations have no desire to quarrel with each other. Nay, they are animated by a very different spirit.

In an interesting article published by the German Socialist paper *Vorwärts*, on September 27, 1914, and reproduced in our Press, occurred the following passage, in which the war is traced to its commercial sources: "Germany has enjoyed an economical prosperity such as no other country has experienced during the last decade. That meant with the capitalist class a revival of strong Imperialist tendencies, which have been evident enough. This, again, gave rise to mistrust abroad, at least in capitalist circles, who did their best to communicate their feelings to the great masses, . . . and so the German people as a whole has been made responsible for what has been the work of a small class. . . . The comrades abroad can be assured that though German workmen are ready to defend their country they will, above all, not forget that their interests are the same as those of the proletariat in other countries, who also against their will were forced into the war and now do their duty. They can rest assured that the German people are not less humane than others—a result to which education through workmen's organizations has greatly contributed. If German soldiers in the excitement of war should commit atrocities, it can be said that among us—and also in other circles—there will not be a single person to approve of them."

Reading this statement—so infinitely more sensible and human than anything to be found in the ordinary Capitalist Press of England and Germany—one cannot help feeling that there is practically little hope for the future *until* the international working masses throughout Europe come forward and, joining hands with each other, take charge of the foolish old Governments (who represent the remains of the decadent feudal and commercial systems), and shape the Western world at last to the heart's desire of the peoples that inhabit it.

"The peoples of the world desire peace," said Bourtzeff, the Russian exile [1]—and he, who has been in many lands, ought to know. But they also—if they would obtain peace—must exercise an eternal vigilance lest they fall into the hands of class-schemers and be betrayed into that which they do *not* desire. The example of Germany—which we

[1] In a letter to the *Times*, September 18, 1914.

have considered above—shows how easily a good and friendly and pacific people may by mere political inattention and ignorance, and by a quasi-scientific philosophy which imposes on its political ignorance, be led into a disastrous situation. It shows how preposterous it is that Governments generally—as at present constituted—should set themselves up as the representatives of the mass-peoples' wishes, and as the arbiters of national destinies. And it shows how vitally necessary it is that the people, even the working masses and the peasants, should have some sort of political education and understanding.

In that matter, of the political education of the masses, America, in her United States and Canada, yields a fine example. Though not certainly perfect, her general standard of education and alertness is infinitely superior to that of the peoples of the Old World. And some writers contend that it is just in that—in her general level and not in her freaks of genius—that America's claim lies to distinction among the nations of the earth. If you consider the peoples of the Old World, whether in England, Scotland, or Ireland, in France, Spain, Italy, Germany, Austria, Russia, or farther East and farther South over the earth, you will find the great masses, on the land or in the workshops, still sunk in vast ignorance, apathy, and irresponsibility. Only here and there among those I have mentioned, and notably among the smaller peoples of Western Europe, like Switzerland, Holland, Denmark, and Sweden, are the masses beginning to stir, as it were, towards the daylight. It can only be with the final opening of their eyes and awakening from slumber that the rule of the classes will be at an end. But that awakening—with the enormous spread of literature and locomotion and intercommunication of all kinds over the modern world, cannot now, one would say, be long delayed.

Meanwhile, and until that era arrives, we can only insist (at any rate in our own country) on a different kind of foreign policy from what we have had—a policy open and strong, not founded on Spread-Eagleism, and decidedly not founded on commercialism and the interests of the trading classes (as the Empire League seem to desire), but directed towards the real welfare of the masses in our own and other lands. If our rulers and representatives really seek peace, here is the obvious way to ensue and secure it—namely, by making political friends of those in all countries who *desire peace* and are already stretching hands of amity to each other. What simpler and more obvious way can there be? "We hail our working-class comrades of every land," says the Manifesto of the Independent Labour Party. "Across the roar of guns we send greeting to the German Socialists. They have laboured unceasingly to promote good relations with Britain, as we with Germany. They are no enemies of ours, but faithful friends. In forcing this appalling crime upon the nations, it is the rulers, the diplomats, the militarists, who have sealed their doom. In tears and blood and bitterness the greater Democracy will be born. With steadfast faith we greet the future; our cause is holy and imperishable, and the labour of our hands has not been in vain."

Yes, we must have a foreign policy strong and sincere—and not only so, but open and avowed. The present Diplomatic system is impossible of continuance. It has grown up in an automatic way out of antiquated conditions, and no one in particular can be blamed for it. But that young men, profoundly ignorant of the world, and having the very *borné* outlook on life which belongs to our gilded youth (67 per cent. of the candidates for the Diplomatic Corps being drawn from Eton alone), having also in high degree that curious want of cosmopolitan sympathy and adaptability which is characteristic of the English wealthy classes (every candidate for the Corps must have at least £400 a year of his own)—that such a type should be charged with the representation of the United Kingdom in foreign affairs is to-day a hopeless anomaly, and indeed a very great danger. The recommendations just published of the Royal Commission are in the right direction, but they need urgent reinforcement and extension by the pressure of public opinion. And if in the present-day situation of affairs we cannot refer every question which arises directly to the nation, we must at least do away with the one-man-Secretary system, and have in his place a large and responsible committee, representative, not of any one party or class but as far as possible of the whole people. [At this moment, for instance, as far as we know, the terms of settlement of the present war may actually be being arranged over our heads, and yet that may be taking place quite apart from the approval and the wishes of the most weighty portion of the nation.]

Another thing that we must look to with some hope for the future is the influence of Women. Profoundly shocked as they are by the senseless folly and monstrous bloodshed of the present conflict, it is certain that when this phase is over they will insist on having a voice in the politics of the future. The time has gone by when the mothers and wives and daughters of the race will consent to sit by meek and silent while the men in their madness are blowing each other's brains out and making mountains out of corpses. It is hardly to be expected that war will cease from the earth this side of the millennium; but women will surely only condone it when urged by some tremendous need or enthusiasm; they will not rejoice –as men sometimes do–in the mere lust of domination and violence. With their keen perception of the little things of life, and the way in which the big things are related to these, they will see too clearly the cost of war in broken hearts and ruined homes to allow their men to embark in it short of the direst necessity.

And through the women I come back to the elementary causes and roots of the present war—the little fibres in our social life which have fed, and are still feeding, the fatal tree whose fruits are, not the healing but the strife of nations. In the present day—though there may be other influences—it is evident enough that rampant and unmeasured commercial greed, concentrating itself in a special class, is the main cause, the tap-root, of the whole business. And this, equally evidently, springs out of the innumerable greed of *individuals*—the countless fibres that combine to one result—the desire of private persons to get rich quick at all costs, to make their gains out of others' losses, to take advantage of each other, to triumph in success regardless of others' failures. And these unworthy motives and inhuman characteristics again spring obviously out of the mean and materialistic ideals of life which still have sway among us—the ideals of wealth and luxury and display—of which the horrors of war are the sure and certain obverse. As long as we foster these things in our private life, so long will they lead in our public life to the embitterment of nation against nation. What is the ruling principle of the interior and domestic conduct of each nation to-day—even within its own borders—but an indecent scramble of class against class, of individual against individual? To rise to noisy power and influence, and to ill-bred wealth and riches, by trampling others down and profiting by their poverty is—as Ruskin long ago told us—the real and prevailing motive of our peoples, whatever their professions of Christianity may be. Small wonder, then, if out of such interior conditions there rise to dominance in the great world those very classes who exhibit the same vulgarities in their most perfect form, and that *their* conflict with each other, as between nation and nation, exhibit to us, in the magnified and hideous form of war, the same sore which is all the time corrupting our internal economy. The brutality and atrocity of modern war is but the reflection of the brutality and inhumanity of our commercial regime and ideals. The slaughter of the battlefields may be more obvious, but it is less deliberate, and it is doubtful whether it be really worse, than the daily and yearly slaughter of the railways, the mines, and the workshops. That being so, it is no good protesting against, and being shocked at, an evil which is our very own creation ; and to cry out against war-lords is useless, when it is *our* desires and ambitions which set the war-lords in motion. Let all those who indulge and luxuriate in ill-gotten wealth to-day (and, indeed, their name is Legion), as well as all those who meanly and idly groan because their wealth is taken from them, think long and deeply on these things.

Truth and simplicity of life are not mere fads ; they are something more than abstractions and private affairs, something more than social ornaments. They are vital matters which lie at the root of national well-being. They are things which in their adoption or in their denial search right through the tissue of public life. To live straightforwardly by your own labour is to be at peace with the world. To live on the labour of others is not only to render your life false at home, but it is to encroach on those around you, to invite resistance and hostility; and when such a principle of life is favoured by a whole people, that people will not only be in a state of internal strife, but will assuredly raise up external enemies on its borders who will seek its destruction.

The working masses and the peasants, whose lives are in the great whole honest—who support themselves (and a good many others besides) by their own labour—*have no quarrel*; and they are the folk who to-day—notwithstanding lies and slanders galore, and much of race-prejudice and ignorance—stretch hands of amity and peace to each other wellnigh all over the world. It is of the modern moneyed classes that we may say that their life-principle (that of taking advantage of others and living on their labour) is essentially false[1]; and these are the classes

[1] There is no reason in itself why Commercialism should be false. Commerce and interchange of goods is of course a perfectly natural and healthy function of social life. Indeed, it is a function which should have a most bene-

which are distinctively the cause of enmities in the modern world, and which, as I have explained above, are able to make use of the military class in order to carry out their designs. It can only be with the ending of the commercial and military classes, as classes, that peace can come to the world. China, founded on the anti-commercial principles of Confucius, disbanded her armies a thousand years ago, and only quite lately —under the frantic menace of Western civilization—felt compelled to reorganize them. She was a thousand years before her time. It can only be with the emergence of a new structure of society, based on the principle of solidarity and mutual aid among the individuals of a nation, and so extending to solidarity and mutual aid among nations, that peace can come to the Western world. It is the best hope of the present war that, like some frightful illness, it marks the working out of deep-seated evils and their ex-

ficent influence in binding nations together. It is when that function is perverted to private gain that it becomes false. But of course without this perversion there would be no distinctively commercial *class* with interests opposed to those of the community.

pulsion from the social organism; and that with its ending the old false civilization, built on private gain, will perish, crushed by its own destructive forces; and in its place the new, the real culture, will arise, founded on the essential unity of mankind.

VII

PATRIOTISM AND INTERNATIONALISM

MANY Socialists and sympathizers with the Labour movement over the world belittle Patriotism, and seem to think that by decrying and discouraging the love of one's country one will bring nearer the day of Internationalism.

I do not agree. Of course we all know there is a lot of sham and false Patriotism—such as, for instance, Pressmongers magnify and make use of in order to sell their papers, or such as comfortable, well-to-do folk with big dividends do so heartily encourage among the poorer classes, who can thus be persuaded to fight for them; we know, indeed, that there is a good deal of very mean and unworthy Patriotism—the flag-waving variety, for instance, which we saw in the

Boer war—exultant over a small nation of farmers defending their homes, and whipped up deliberately by a commercial gang for their own purposes; or the narrow-minded, lying, canting variety which blinds a people to its own faults, and credits itself with all the moral virtues, while at the same time it gloats over every defamation of the enemy. There is a good deal of that variety in the present war. And it is easy to understand that many people, sick of that sort of Patriotism, would go straight for a ready-made denial of all frontiers and boundaries.

Still, allowing to the full all that can be said in the above direction, one must admit also that there is such a thing as a true Patriotism, and I do not see why—however socialist or cosmopolitan we may be—we should not recognize what is an obvious fact. There is a love of one's own country—a genuine attachment to and preference for it—" in spite of all temptations to belong to other nations "—which after all is very natural, and on the whole a sound and healthy thing. There may be some people whose minds are so lofty that to them all peoples and races are alike and without preference ; but one knows that the vast multitudes of our mortal earth are not made like that. "If a man love not his brother whom he hath seen, how shall he love God whom he hath not seen?" It is certainly easier and more natural to make an effort and a sacrifice for the sake of your own countrymen whom you know so well and with whom you are linked by a thousand ties than for the sake of foreigners who are little more than a name—however worthy you may honestly believe the latter to be. It is more obvious and instinctive for a man to work for his own family than to give his services to his municipality or his county council. Charity begins at home, and the wider spirit of human love and helpfulness which passes beyond the narrow bounds of the family hearth has perhaps to find an intermediate sphere before it can unfold itself and expand in the great field of Humanity among all colours and races.

Personally, I am probably more International by temperament than Patriotic. I feel a strange kinship and intimacy with all sorts of queer and outlandish races—Chinese, Egyptian, Mexican, or Polynesian—and always a slight but persistent sense of estrangement and misapprehension among my own people. Flag-waving certainly does not stir me. Still, I feel that, whatever one's country may be, the love of it has value and is not to be scoffed at. The Nation is bigger than the Parish; and to a man of limited outlook it is a means of getting him out of his own very narrow and local circle of life; to rob him of that in order to jump him into a cosmopolitan attitude (which to him may be quite empty and arid) is a mistake. It is easy enough to break the shell for the growing chick, but if you break it too soon your chick, when hatched, will be dead.

If you look at the great majority of those who are enthusing just now about our country and patriotically detesting the Germans, you will see that notwithstanding lies and slanders and cant galore, and much of conceit and vanity, their patriotism *is* pulling them together from one end of Britain to another, causing them to help each other in a thousand ways, urging them to make sacrifices for the common good, helping them to grow the sinews and limbs of the body politic, and even the wings which will one day transport that body into a bigger world. Really, I think we ought to be very grateful to the Germans for doing all this for us; and the Germans ought to be grateful to us for an exactly similar reason. You will see plainly enough that the great majority of those who are at this moment giving their thoughts and lives for their countrymen and neighbours either in Germany or in England could not by any manner of possibility be expected to act with similar self-surrender and enthusiasm in an International cause. They are not grown to that point of development yet, and it is better that they should learn helpfulness and brotherhood within somewhat narrow bounds than perhaps not learn these things at all in the open and indiscriminate field of universal equality. After all, to stimulate love and friendship there is nothing like a common enemy!

It is an old story and an old difficulty. There comes a time when every institution of social life becomes rotten and diseased and has to be removed to make way for the new life which is expanding behind it. Broadly speaking, we may say that the institution of Patriotism is *approaching* this period—at any rate over Western Europe. The outlines of an International life are becoming clearly visible behind it.

What we have to do is to help on that international life and spirit to our best, and certainly clear out a lot of sham patriotism that stands in its way; but this has to be done with discrimination and a certain tact. People must be made to see that "my country, right or wrong," is not the genuine article. They must be made to understand how easily this sort of slapdash sentiment throws them into the hands of scheming politicians and wire-pullers for sinister purposes—how readily it can be made use of directly it has become a mere unreasoning instinct and habit. If a war is wanted, or conscription, or a customs tariff—it may be merely to suit the coward fears of autocratic rulers, or the selfish interests of some group of contractors or concession-hunters—all that the parties concerned have to do is to play the patriotic stop, and they stand a good chance of getting what they want. Just now there is a good bit of fleecing going on in this fashion—both of the public and the wage-workers. Even in its more healthy forms, when delayed in too long, patriotism easily becomes morbid and delays also the birth of the larger spirit which is waiting behind it. The Continental Socialists complain that their cause has hitherto made little progress in Alsace-Lorraine and Poland for the simple reason that political circumstances have over-accentuated the patriotic devotion in both these regions.

Thus we have to push on with discrimination. Always we have to remember that the wide, free sense of equality and kinship which lies at the root of Internationalism is the real goal, and that the other thing is but a step on the way, albeit a necessary step. Always we have to press on towards that great and final liberation—the realization of our common humanity, the recognition of the same great soul of man slumbering under all forms in the heart of all races—the one guarantee and assurance of the advent of World-peace.

That we are verging rapidly towards some altered perspective I quite believe; and the day is coming when in the social and political spheres International activity will make excessive patriotism seem somewhat ridiculous —as, in fact, it has already done in the spheres of Science and Industry and Art. Still, I also do not see any reason why the two tendencies should not work side by side. The health of local organs and members in the human body is by no means incompatible with the health of the whole organism, and we may understand the great map of Humanity all the better for its being differently coloured in different parts.

VIII

THE PSYCHOLOGY OF WAR AND RECRUITING

November, 1914.

I SOMETIMES think the country-folk round about where I live the most sensible people I know. They say with regard to the War—or said at its outset: " What are they fighting about? *I* can't make out, and nobody seems to know. What I've seen o' the Germans they're a decent enough folk—much like ourselves. If there's got to be fightin, why don't them as makes the quarrel go and fight wi' each other? But killing all them folk that's got no quarrel, and burnin' their houses and farms, and tramplin' down all that good corn-and all them brave men dead what can never live again-its scandalous, I say."

This at the outset. But afterwards, when

the papers had duly explained that the Germans were mere barbarians and savages, bent on reducing the whole world to military slavery, they began to take sides and feel there was good cause for fighting. Meanwhile almost exactly the same thing was happening in Germany, where England was being represented as a greedy and deceitful Power, trying to boss and crush all the other nations. Thus each nation did what was perhaps, from its own point of view, the most sensible thing to do—persuaded itself that it was fighting in a just and heroic cause, that it was a St. George against the Dragon, a David out to slay Goliath.

The attitude of the peasant, however, or agriculturist, all over the world, is the same. He does not deal in romantic talk about St. George and the Dragon. He sees too clearly the downright facts of life. He has no interest in fighting, and he does not want to fight. Being the one honest man in the community—the one man who creates, not only his own food but the food of others besides, and who knows the value of his work, he perceives without illusion the foolery of War, the hideous waste of it, the shocking toll of agony and loss which it inflicts—and if left to himself would as a rule have no hand in it. It is only occasionally—when ground down beyond endurance by the rent-racking classes above him, or threatened beyond endurance by an enemy from abroad, that he turns his reaping-hook into a sword and his muck-fork into a three-pronged bayonet, exchanges his fowling-piece for a rifie, and fights savagely for his home and his bit of a field.

England, curiously enough, is almost the only country in the world where the peasant or ordinary field-worker *has* no field of his own ; and I find that in the villages and among the general agricultural population there is even now but little enthusiasm for

In Servia, for instance, which many folk doubtless regard as a benighted country, more than four-fifths of the people are peasant farmers and cultivate lands belonging to their own families. "These holdings cannot be sold or mortgaged entire ; the law forbids the alienation for debt of a peasant's cottage, his garden or courtyard, his plough, the last few acres of his land, and the cattle necessary for working his farm." [Encycl. Brit.] In 1910 there were altogether *five hundred* agricultural co-operative societies in Servia.

the present war–though the raid on our coasts at Scarborough and other places certainly did something to stimulate it. Partly this is, as I have said, because the agricultural worker knows that his work is foundational, and that nothing else is of importance compared with it. [At this moment, for instance, there are peasants in Belgium and Northern France ploughing and sowing, and so forth, actually close to the trenches and between the fighting lines.] Partly it is because in England, alas! the countryman *has* so little right or direct interest in the soil. One wonders sometimes why he *should* feel any enthusiasm. Why should men want to fight for their land when they have no land to fight for–when the most they can do is to die at the foot of a trespass-board, singing, "Britons never, never shall be slaves!"

If the War is ever finished, surely one of the first things to be insisted on afterwards, with regard to England, must be the settlement of the actual people (not the parasites) on the land. Else how, after all that they have gone through, can it be expected that they will ever again "fight for their country"? But that this vast landless population in the villages and country districts–hungering as it is for some sure tenure and interest in the soil–should actually, as now, be berated and scolded by superior persons of the "upper" classes, and threatened with conscription if it does not "come forward" more readily, is a spectacle sufficient to gratify the most hardened cynic.

Certainly it is remarkable that such numbers of the great working masses of this country (including villagers) should come forward in connexion with the war, and join the standard and the ranks of fighting men–as they do–and it is a thing for which one must honour them. But in that matter there are not a few considerations to be kept in mind.

In the first place a large number are not really very enthusiastic, but simply join because pressure to do so is put upon them by their "masters." The press-gangs of old exist no longer, but substitutes for them revive in subtler form. Many large landlords, for instance, have given notice to a percentage of their gamekeepers, gardeners, park employees, and the like, to the effect that their services are no longer required, but that if they enlist in the ranks now they will be reinstated in their masters' service again when the war is over ("if still alive" is, we presume, understood). Large numbers of manufacturing and other firms have notified their workmen and clerks in similar terms. This means pretty serious economic pressure. A man in the prime of life, suddenly ousted from his job, and with no prospect either of finding a similar job elsewhere or of learning any new one, is in a pretty fix. His only certain refuge lies in the fact that he can be taught to use a rifle in a few weeks; and in a few weeks perhaps it becomes clear to him that to accept that offer and the pay that goes with it–poor as it is–is his only chance.

There are others, again–perhaps a very large number–who do not care much about the war in itself, and probably have only the vaguest notion of what it is all about, but for them to join the ranks means adventure, comradeship, the open air–all fascinating things; and they hail the prospect with joy as an escape from intolerable dullness–from the monotony of the desk and the stuffy office, from the dreary round and mechanical routine of the factory bench, from the depressing environment of "home" and domestic squalor.

I must confess—though I have no general prejudice in favour of war—that I have been much struck, since the outbreak of the present one, by the altered look of crowds of young men whom I personally know—who are now drilling or otherwise preparing for it. The gay look on their faces, the blood in their cheeks, the upright carriage and quick, elate step—when compared with the hang-dog, sallow, dull creatures I knew before—all testify to the working of some magic influence.

As I say, I do not think that this influence in most cases has much to do with enthusiasm for the "cause" or any mere lust of "battle" (happily indeed for the most part they do not for a moment realize what modern battle means). It is simply escape from the hateful conditions of present-day commercialism and its hideous wage-slavery into something like the normal life of young manhood—a life in the open under the wide sky, blood-stirring enterprise, risk if you will, co-operation and *camaraderie*. These are the inviting, beckoning things, the things which swing the balance down—even though hardships, low pay, and high chances of injury and death are thrown in the opposite scale.

Nevertheless, and despite these other considerations, there does certainly remain, in this as in other wars, a fair number of men among those who enlist who are *bonâ fide* inspired by some Ideal which they feel to be worth fighting for. It may be Patriotism or love of their country; it may be "to put down militarism"; it may be Religion or Honour or what not. And it is fine that it should be so. They may in cases be deluded, or mistaken about facts; the ideal they fight for may be childish (as in the mediæval Crusades); still, even so it is fine that people should be willing to give their lives for an idea—that they should be capable of being inspired by a vision. Humanity has at least advanced as far as that.

I suppose patriotism, or love of country—when it comes to its full realization, as in the case of invasion by an enemy, is the most powerful and tremendous of such ideals, sweeping everything before it. It represents something ingrained in the blood. In that case all the other motives for fighting—economic or what not—disappear and are swallowed up. Material life and social conditions under a German government might externally be as comfortable and prosperous as under our own, but for most of us something in the soul would wither and sicken at the thought.

Anyhow, whatever the motives may be which urge *individuals* into war—whether sheer necessity or patriotism, or the prospect of wages or distinction, or the love of adventure—a nation or a people in order to fight *must* have a " cause " to fight for, something which its public opinion, its leaders, and its Press can appropriate—some phrase which it can inscribe on its shield: be it " Country " or " God " or " Freedom from Tyranny," or " Culture *versus* Barbarism." It must have some such cry, else obviously it could not fight with any whole-heartedness or any force.

The thing is a psychological necessity. Every one, when he gets into a quarrel, justifies himself and accuses the other party.

He puts his own conduct in an ideal light, and the conduct of his opponent in the reverse! Doubtless if we were all angels and could impartially enter into all the origins of the quarrel, we should not fight, because to "understand" would be to "forgive"; but as we have not reached that stage, and as we cannot even explain why we are quarrelling–the matter being so complex–we are fain to adopt a phrase and fight on the strength of that. It is useless to call this hypocrisy. It is a psychological necessity. It is the same necessity which makes a mistress dismiss her maid on the score of a broken teapot, though really she has no end of secret grievances against her; or which makes the man of science condense the endless complexity of certain physical phenomena into a neat but lying formula which he calls a *Law of Nature*. He could not possibly give all the real facts, and so he uses a phrase.

In war, therefore, each nation adopts a motto as its reason for fighting. Sometimes the two opposing nations both adopt the same motto! England and Germany both inscribe on their banners: "Culture *versus*

Barbarism." Each believes in its own good faith, and each accuses the other of hypocrisy.

In a sense this is all right, and could not be better. It does not so much matter which is really the most cultured nation, England or Germany, as that each should really *believe* that it is fighting in the cause of Culture. Then, so fighting for what it knows to be a good cause, the wounds and death endured and the national losses and depletion are not such sad and dreadful things as they at first appear. They liberate the soul of the individual; they liberate the soul of the nation. They are sacrifices made for an ideal; and (provided they are truly such) the God within is well-pleased and comes one step nearer to his incarnation. Whatever inner thing you make sacrifices for, the same will in time appear visibly in your life–blessing or cursing you. Therefore, beware! and take good care as to what that inner thing really is.

Such is the meaning of the use of a phrase or "battle-cry"; but we have, indeed, to be on our guard against *how* we use it. It can so easily become a piece of cant or hypocrisy. It can so easily be engineered by ruling cliques and classes for their own purposes–to persuade and compel the people to fight *their* battles. The politicians get us (for reasons which they do not explain) into a nice little entanglement–perhaps with some tribe of savages, perhaps with a great European Power; and before the nation knows where it is it finds itself committed to a campaign which may develop and become a serious war. Then there is no alternative but for Ministers to repair to a certain Cabinet where the well-dried formulæ they need are kept hanging, and select one for their use. It may be "Women and Children," or it may be "Immoral Savages," or it may be "Empire," or it may be "Our Word of Honour." Having selected the right one, and duly displayed and advertised it, they have little difficulty in making the nation rise to the bait, and fight whatever battles they desire.

Since the early beginnings of the human race we can perceive the same processes in operation. We can almost guess the grade of advancement reached among primitive tribes by simply taking note of their *totems*. These were emblems of the things which held the mind of the tribe, as admirable or terrible, with which it was proud to identify itself—the fox, for instance, or the bear, the kangaroo, or the eagle. To be worthy of *such ideals* men fought. Later, every little people, every knightly family, every group of adventurers, adopted a device for its shield, a motto for its flag, a figure of some kind, human, or more often animal. Even the modern nations have not got much farther; and we can judge of *their* stage of advancement by the beasts of prey they flaunt on their banners or the deep-throat curses which resound in their national anthems.

But surely the time has now come—even with this world-war—when the great heart of the peoples will wake up to the savagery and the folly perpetrated in their names. The people, who, although they enjoy a " scrap " now and then, are essentially peaceful, essentially friendly, all the world over; who in the intervals of slaughter offer cigarettes to their foes, and tenderly dress their enemies' wounds; whose worst and agelong sin it is that they allow themselves so easily to be dominated and led by ambitious and greedy schemers—surely it is time that they should wake up and throw off these sham governments—these governments that are three-quarters class-scheming and fraud and only one-quarter genuine expressions of public spirit—and declare the heart of solidarity that is within them.

The leaders and high priests of the world have used the name of Christianity to bless their own nefarious works with, till the soul is sick at the very sound of the word; but surely the time has come when the peoples themselves out of their own heart will proclaim the advent of the Son of Man—conscious of it, indeed, as a great light of brotherhood shining within them, even amid the clouds of race-enmity and ignorance, and will deny once for all the gospel of world-empire and conquest which has so long been foisted on them for insidiously selfish ends.

An empire based on brotherhood—a holy *human* empire of the World, including all races and colours in a common unity and equality—yes! But these shoddy empires based on militarism and commercialism, and built up in order to secure the unclean ascendancy of two outworn and effete classes over the rest of mankind—a thousand times no! That dispensation, thank Heaven! is past. "These fatuous empires with their parade of power and their absolute lack of any real policy—this British Lion, this Russian Bear, these German, French, and American Eagles—these birds and beasts of prey—with their barbaric notions of Greed and War, their impossible armaments, and their swift financial ruin impending—will fall and be rent asunder. The hollow masks of them will perish. And the sooner the better. But underneath surely there will be rejoicing, for it will be found that so after all the real peoples of the earth have come one degree nearer together—yes, one degree nearer together."

IX

CONSCRIPTION

December, 1914.

WHILE protesting, as I have already done, against forced military service, it must still be admitted that the argument in favour of it retains a certain validity: to the extent, namely, that every one owes a duty of some kind to his own people, that it is mean to accept all the advantages of citizenship security, protection, settled conditions of life, and so forth—and still to refuse to make sacrifice for one's country in a time of distress or danger. It is difficult of course for any one to trace all the threads and fibres which have worked themselves into his life from his own homeland—as it is difficult for a child to trace all the qualities of blood that it owes to its mother; but there they are, and though some of these native inheritances and conditions may not really be to a man's liking, yet he can hardly refuse to acknowledge them, or to confess the debt of gratitude that he owes to the land of his birth.

Granting all this, however, most fully, there still remains a long stretch from this admission to that of forced military service. The drawbacks to this latter are many. In the first place compulsion anyhow is bad. A voluntary citizen army may be all right; but to *compel* a man to fight, whether he will or not—in violation, perhaps, of his conscience, of his instinct, of his temperament—is an inexcusable outrage on his rights as a human being. In the second place it is gross folly; for a man who fights devoid of freewill and against his conscience, against his temperament, cannot possibly make a good fighter. An army of such recusants, however large, would be useless; and even a few mixed with the others do, as a matter of fact, greatly lower the efficiency of the whole force associated with them. In the third place compulsion means compulsion by a Government, and Government, at any rate to-day, means class-rule. Forced military service means service under and subjection to a Class. That means Wars carried on abroad to serve the interests, often iniquitous enough, of the Few; and military operations entered into at home to suppress popular discontent or to confirm class-power. To none of these things could any high-minded man of democratic temper consent. There are other drawbacks, but these will do to begin with.

On the other hand, if we reject enforced militarism are we to throw overboard the idea of "national service" altogether?

I think not. The way out is fairly clear and obvious. Let it be understood that there *is* such a thing as national or public service, to which (within the limits of individual conscience and capacity) every one is bound to respond. Let it be understood that at a certain age, say from sixteen to eighteen (but the period would no doubt be a movable one) every one, boy or girl, rich or poor, shall go through a course of training fitting him or her for healthy and effective citizenship. This would include *first of all* bodily exercises and drill (needed by almost all, but especially in the present day by town workers), all sorts of scouting-work, familiarity with Nature, camp and outdoor life; then all kinds of elementary and necessary trades, like agriculture in some form or other, metal-work, wood-work, cloth-work, tailoring, bootmaking; then such things as rifle-shooting, ambulance-work, nursing, cookery, and so on. Let it be understood that *every one*, male or female, rich or poor, learned or ignorant, is expected to qualify—not in the whole programme, but first of all and as far as humanly possible in the primary condition of physical health and development, and then after that in some one, at any rate, of the above-mentioned or similar trades—so that in case of general need or distress he can do *something* of use. That would at least be an approach to a valuable and reasonable institution.

As things are it is appalling to think of the abject futility and *uselessness* of vast classes in all the modern nations of to-day—but perhaps especially in our own nation. Think of the populations of our drawing-rooms, of our well-to-do clubs, of our universities, of our commercial and professional offices, whose occupations, whatever they are, are entirely remote from the direct needs and meanings of life; or again of the vast masses who inhabit the mean streets of our great towns, ignorant, ill-grown, unskilled, and in a chronic state of most precarious and uncertain employment. What would these populations do in any case of national crisis – say in a case of serious war or famine or huge bankruptcy of trade or multitudinous invasion by Chinese or Japanese, or of total collapse of credit and industry? With a few brilliant exceptions they would collapse too. They could not feed themselves, clothe themselves, or defend themselves; they could not build shelters from the storm, or make tools or weapons of any kind for their own use; they would be unable to nurse each other in illness or cook for each other in health. A tribe of Arabs or a commando of Boer farmers would be far more competent than they.

But the said deficiency, which would be painfully illustrated by a serious crisis, is there equally in ordinary humdrum times of peace. The crippled and idiotic life which would bring disaster *then* is undermining our very existence *now*. Is it not time that a sensible nation should look to it that every one of its members, when adult, should at least be healthy, well-fed, and well-grown, and that each should not only be decently developed in himself or herself, but should be capable of bearing a useful part of some kind in the life of the nation? Is it not time that the nation should place *first of all* on its programme the creation of capable and healthy citizens? Can a nation be really effective, really strong, really secure, without this? I do not seem to doubt a large *willingness* among our people to-day for mutual service and helpfulness—I believe a vast number of our young women of the well-to-do type are at this moment deeply regretting their inability to do anything except knit superfluous mufflers—but was there ever in the history of the world such huge, such wide-flooding *incompetence*? The willingness of the well-to-do classes may be judged from their readiness to come forward with subscriptions, their incompetence from the fact that they have *nothing else to offer*: that is, that all they can offer is to set *some one else* (by means of their money) to do useful work in their place.

They cannot themselves nurse wounded soldiers, or make boots for them, or build huts or weave blankets; they cannot help in housing or building schemes, or in schemes for the reclaiming and cultivation of waste lands; they cannot grow corn or bake bread or cook simple meals for the assistance of the indigent or the aged or the feeble, because they understand none of these things; but they can *pay some one else* to do them—that is, they can divert some of the money, which they have already taken from the workers, to setting the latter toiling again! But what use would that be on the day when our monetary system broke down—as it nearly did at the commencement of this war? What use would it be on some critical day when a hostile invasion called every competent man and woman to do the work of defence absolutely necessary at the moment? What use would it be in the hour when complete commercial dislocation caused downright famine? Who would look at offers of money then? Could the nation carry this vast mass of incompetents and idlers on its back then; and can it reasonably be expected to do so now?

A terrible and serious crisis, as I have already said, awaits us—even when the War is over—a crisis probably worse than that which we are passing through now. We have to remember the debts that are being piled up. If the nations are staggering along now under the enormous load of idlers and parasites living on interest, how will it be then? Unless we can reorganize our Western societies on a real foundation of actual life, of practical capacity, of honest and square living, and of mutual help instead of mutual robbery, they will infallibly collapse, or pass into strange and alien hands. Now is the critical moment when with the enormous powers of production which we wield it may be possible to make a new start, and base the social life of the future on a generous recognition of the fellowship of all. How many times have the civilizations of the past, ignoring this salvation, gone down into the gulf! Can we find a better hope for our civilization to-day?

It is clear, I think, that any nation that wants to stand the shock of events in the future, and to hold its own in the vast flux of racial and political changes which is coming on the world, will have to found its life, not on theories and views, or on the shifting sands of literature and fashion, but on the solid rock of the real *material* capability of its citizens, and on their willingness, their readiness to help each other—their ingrained instinct of mutual service. A conscript army, forced upon us by a government and becoming inevitably a tool for the use of a governing class, we do not want and we will not have; but a nation of capable men and women, who know what life is and are prepared to meet it at all points–who will in many cases make a free gift of their capital and land for such purposes as I have just outlined —we *must* have. Personally I would not even here—though the need is a crying one—advocate downright compulsion; but I would make these things a part of the recognized system of education, with appropriate regulations and the strongest recommendations and inducements to every individual to fall in and co-operate with them. Thus in time an urgent public opinion might be formed which would brand as disgraceful the conduct of any person who refused to qualify himself for useful service, or who, when qualified, deliberately refused to respond to the call for such service, if needed. Under such conditions the question of military defence would solve itself. Thousands and thousands of men would of their own free choice at an early age and during a certain period qualify themselves in military matters; other thousands, men and women, would qualify in nursing or ambulance work; other millions, again, would be prepared to aid in transport work, or in the production of food, clothing, shelter, and the thousand and one necessaries of life. No one would be called upon to do work which he had not chosen, no one would be forced to take up an activity which was hateful to him, yet all would feel that what they could do and did do would be helpful to the other ranks and ranges, and would be *solidaire* with the rest of the nation. Such a nation would be sane and prosperous in time of peace, and absolutely safe and impregnable in the hour of danger.

X

HOW SHALL THE PLAGUE BE STAYED?

Christmas, 1914.

PEOPLE ask what new arrangements of diplomacy or revivals of Christianity—what alliances, *ententes*, leagues of peace, Hague tribunals, regulation of armaments, weeks of prayer, or tons of Christmas puddings sent into the enemies' camps—will finally scotch this pestilence of war. And there is no answer, because the answer is too close at hand for us to see it.

Nothing but the general abandonment of the system of living on the labour of others will avail. *There is no other way*. This, whether as between individuals or as between nations, is—and has been since the beginning of the world—the root-cause of war. Early and primitive wars were for this—to raid crops and cattle, to carry off slaves on whose toil the conquerors could subsist; and the latest wars are the same. To acquire rubber concessions, gold-mines, diamond-mines, where coloured labour may be exploited to its bitterest extreme; to secure colonies and outlying lands, where giant capitalist enterprises (with either white or coloured labour) may make huge dividends out of the raising of minerals and other industrial products; to crush any other Power which stands in the way of these greedy and inhuman ambitions—such are the objects of wars to-day. And we do not see the cause of the sore because it is so near to us, because it is in our blood. The whole private life of the commercial and capitalist classes (who stand as the representatives of the nations to-day) is founded on the same principle. As individuals our one object is to find some worker or group of workers whose labour value we can appropriate. Look at the endless columns of stock and share quotations in the daily papers, and consider the armies of those who scan these lists over their breakfast-tables with the one view of finding somewhere an industrial concern whose slave-driven toilers will yield the shareholder 5, 6, 7, 8, 10, 12 per cent. on his capital. Undisguised and shameless parasitism is the order, or disorder, of our days. The rapacity of beasts of prey is in our social life but thinly veiled—thinly veiled indeed by a wash of "Christian" sentiment and by a network of philanthropic institutions for the supposed benefit of the very victims whom we have robbed.

Is it any wonder that this principle of internecine warfare and rapacity which rules in our midst, this vulgar greed, which loads people's bodies with jewels and furs and their tables with costly food, regardless of those from whom these comforts are snatched, should eventuate ultimately in rapacity and violence on the vast stage of the drama of nations, and in red letters of war and conflict written across the continents? It is no good, with a pious snuffle, to say we are out to put down warfare and militarism, and all the time to encourage in our own lives, and in our Church and Empire Leagues and other institutions, the most sordid and selfish commercialism—

which itself is in essence a warfare, only a warfare of a far meaner and more cowardly kind than that which is signalized by the shock of troops or the rage of rifles and cannon.

No, there is no other way; and only by the general abandonment of our present commercial and capitalist system will the plague of war be stayed.[1]

[1] When these hundreds and hundreds of thousands of men return home after the war is over, do we expect them to go meekly back to the idiotic slavery of dingy offices and dirty workshops? If we do I trust that we shall be disappointed. These men who have fought so nobly for their land, and who have tasted, even under the most trying conditions, something of the largeness and gladness of a free open-air life, will, I hope, refuse to knuckle down again to the old commercialism. Now at last arises the opportunity for our outworn Civilization to make a fresh start. Now comes the chance to establish great self-supporting Colonies in our own countrysides and co-operative concerns where real Goods may be manufactured and Agriculture carried on in free and glad and healthy industry.

XI

COMMERCIAL PROSPERITY THE PROSPERITY OF A CLASS

THE economics of the statement that "commercial prosperity means little more than the prosperity of a *class*"[1] may be roughly indicated by the following considerations: International trade means division of labour among the nations. There is certainly a gain in such division, a margin of advantage in production; and that gain, that margin, is secured by the trading class. That is all.

Let us take an example, and to simplify the problem let us leave out of account those exotic products—like tea or rubber or raw cotton—which *can* only be produced in one of the exchanging countries. Let us take the case of Germany and England, both pro-

[1] See p. 50 above.

ducing cutlery and both producing cloth. There is no reason why each country should not produce *both* articles exclusively for its own use; and as a matter of fact for a long time they did so. But presently it was found that the cost of production of certain kinds of cutlery was less in Germany, and the cost of production of certain kinds of cloth less in England. Merchants and dealers came in and effected the exchange, and so an intertrade has sprung up. The effect of this on the workers in England is simply to transfer a certain amount of employment from the cutlery trade to the cloth trade, and on the workers in Germany to transfer an equal amount from the cloth trade to the cutlery trade. This may mean dislocation of industry; but the actual number of persons employed or of wages received in both countries may in such a case remain just the same as before. There is nothing in the mere fact of exchange to alter those figures. There is, however, a gain, there is a marginal advantage, in the exchange; and that is collared by the merchants and dealers. It is, in fact, *in order to secure this margin* that the merchant class arises. This is, of course, a very simple and elementary statement of the problem, and the exceptions to it or modifications of it may be supplied by the reader. But in the main it embodies the very obvious truth that trade is created for the advantage of the trader (who often also in modern times is the manufacturer himself). What advantages may here and there leak through to the public or to the employee are small and, so to speak, accidental. The mere fact of exchange in itself forms no index of general prosperity. Yet it is often assumed that it does. If, for instance, it should happen that the whole production of cutlery, as between Germany and England, were secured by Germany, and the whole production of cloth were secured by England, so that the *whole* of these products on each side had to be exchanged, then doubtless there would be great jubilation–talk of the immense growth of oversea trade in both countries, the wonderful increase of exports and imports, the great prosperity, and so forth; but really and obviously it would only mean the jubilation and the prosperity of the merchants, the brokers, the railway and shipping companies of both lands. There would be an increase in *their* riches (and an increase in the number of their employees). It would mean more merchant palaces in Park Lane, bigger dividends on the shares of transport companies; but after that the general position of the manual workers in both trades, the numbers employed, and their rates of wages would be much as before. Prices also, as regards the general Public, would be but little altered. It is only because this great trading, manufacturing, and commercial class has amassed such enormous wealth and influence, and is able to command the Press, and social position, and votes and representation on public bodies and in both Houses of Parliament, that it succeeds in impressing the nation generally with the idea that *its* welfare is the welfare of the whole people, and its prosperity the advantage of every citizen. And it is in this very fact that its great moral and social danger to the community lies.

It must not be thought (but I believe I have said this before) that in making out that the commercial classes are largely to blame for modern wars I mean to say that the present war, and many previous ones, have been *directly* instigated by commercial folk. It is rather that the atmosphere of commercial competition and rivalry automatically leads up to military rivalries and collisions, which often at the last moment (though not always) turn out contrary to the wishes of the commercial people themselves. Also I would repeat that it is not *Commerce* but the *class* interest that is to blame. Commerce and exchange, as we know in a thousand ways, have the effect of drawing peoples together, giving them common interests, acquaintance, and understanding of each other, and so making for peace. The great jubilation during the latter half of the nineteenth century–from 1851 onwards—over world-wide trade and Industrial Exhibitions, as the heralds of the world's peace and amity–a jubilation voiced in Tennyson's earlier *Locksley Hall*—was to a certain extent justified. There is no doubt that the nations have been drawn together by intertrading and learned to know each other. Bonds, commercial and personal, have grown up between them, and are growing up, which must inevitably make wars more difficult in the future and less desirable. And if it had been possible to carry on this intertrade in a spirit of real friendliness and without grasping or greed the result to-day would be incalculably great. But, unfortunately, this latter element came in to an extent quite unforeseen and blighted the prophetic hopes. The second *Locksley Hall* was a wail of disillusionment. The growth of large mercantile classes, intoxicated with wealth and pursuing their own interests *apart from, and indeed largely in opposition to,* those of the mass-peoples, derailed the forward movement, and led in some of the ways which I have indicated above to more of conflict between the nations and less of peace.

Doubtless the growth of these mercantile classes has to a certain extent been inevitable; and we must do them the justice to acknowledge that their enterprise and ingenuity (even set in action for their own private advantage) have been of considerable benefit to the world, and that their growth may represent a necessary stage in affairs. Still, we cannot help looking forward to a time when, this stage having been completed, and commerce between nation and nation having ceased to be handled for mere private profit and advantage, the parasitical power in our midst which preys upon the Commonweal will disappear, the mercantile classes will become organic with the Community, and one great and sinister source of wars will also cease.

XII

COLONIES AND SEAPORTS

THERE is another point of economics on which there seems to be some confusion of mind. If mere extension of Trade is the thing sought for, it really does not matter much, in these days of swift and international transport, whether the outlying lands with which the Trader deals or the ports *through* which he deals are the property of his own nation or of some other nation. The trade goes on all the same. England certainly has colonies all over the world; but with her free trade and open ports it often happens that one of her colonies takes more German or French goods of a certain class than English goods of the same class; or that it exports more to Germany and France than it does to England. The bulk, for instance, of the produce of our West African colonies goes, in normal times, to Germany. German or French trade does not suffer in dealing with English colonies, though English trade may sometimes suffer in dealing with French, German or other foreign colonies on account of the preferential duties they put on in favour of their own goods. Except for these tariff-walls and bounty systems (which after all, on account of their disturbing and crippling effect, seem to be gradually going out of fashion) trade flows over the world, regardless of national barriers, and will continue so to flow. It is all a question of relative efficiency and price. German goods, owing to their cheapness and their accuracy of construction, have of late years been penetrating everywhere; and to the German trader, as a pure matter of trade, it makes no difference whether he sells to a foreign nation or a German colony.

It is the same with seaports. Holland is delighted to provide passage for Germany's exports and imports, and probably does so at a minimum cost. The Berlin manufacturer or merchant would be no better off, as far as trade conditions are concerned, if Germany instead of Holland held the mouths of the Rhine. The same with a harbour like Salonika. Germany or Austria may covet dreadfully its possession; and for strategic or political reasons they may be right, but for pure trade purposes Salonika in the hands of the Greeks would probably (except for certain initial expenses in the enlargement of dock accommodation) serve them as well as in their own hands.

Of course there *are* other reasons which make nations desire colonies and ports. Such things may be useful for offensive or defensive purposes against other nations; they feed a jealous sense of importance and Imperialism; they provide outlets for population and access to lands where the institutions and customs of the Homeland prevail; they supply financiers with a field for the investment of capital under the protection of their own Governments; they favour the development of a national *carrying* trade; and, above all, they supply plentiful official and other posts and situations for the young men of the middle and commercial classes; but for the mere extension and development of the nation's general trade and commerce it is doubtful whether they have anything like the importance commonly credited to them.

XIII

WAR AND THE SEX IMPULSE

January, 1915.

IT seems that War, like all greatest things—like Passion, Politics, Religion, and so forth—is impossible to reckon up. It belongs to another plane of existence than our ordinary workaday life, and breaks into the latter as violently and unreasonably as a volcano into the cool pastures where cows and sheep are grazing. No arguments, protests, proofs, or explanations are of any avail; and those that are advanced are confused, contradictory, and unconvincing. Just as people quarrel most violently over Politics and Religion, because, in fact, those are the two subjects which no one really understands, so they quarrel in Warfare, not really knowing *why*, but impelled by deep, inscrutable forces. Spectators even and neutrals, for the same reason, take sides and range themselves bitterly, if only in argument, against each other.

But Logic and Morals are of no use on these occasions. They are too thin. They are only threads in a vast fabric. You extract a single thread from the weaving of a carpet, and note its colour and its concatenations, but that gives you no faintest idea of the pattern of the carpet; and then you extract another, and another, but you are no nearer the design. Logic and morals are similar threads in the great web of life. You may follow them in various directions, but without effective result. Life is so much greater than either; and War is a volcanic manifestation of Life which gives them little or no heed.

There is a madness of nations, as well as of individual people. Every one who has paid attention to the fluctuations of popular sentiment knows how strange, how unaccountable, these are. They seem to suggest the coming to the surface, from time to time, of hidden waves–groundswells of some deep ocean. The temper, the temperament, the character, the policy of a whole nation will change, and it is difficult to see why. Sometimes a passion, a fury, a veritable mania, quite unlike its ordinary self, will seize it. There is a madness of peoples, which causes them for a while to hate each other with bitter hatred, to fight furiously and wound and injure each other; and then lo! a little while more and they are shaking hands and embracing and swearing eternal friendship! What does it all mean?

It is all as mad and unreasonable as Love is—and that is saying a good deal! In love, too, people desire to *hurt* each other; they do not hesitate to wound one another—wounding hearts, wounding bodies even, and hating themselves even while they act so. What does it all mean? Are they trying the one to reach the other *at all costs*—if not by embraces, at least by injuries—each longing to make his or her personality felt, to *impress* himself or herself upon the other in such wise as never again to be forgotten. Sometimes a man will stab the girl he loves, if he cannot get at her any other way. Sex itself is a positive battle. Lust connects itself only too frequently with violence and the spilling of blood.

Is it possible that something the same happens with whole nations and peoples—an actual lust and passion of conflict, a mad intercourse and ravishment, a kind of generation in each other, and exchange of life-essences, leaving the two peoples thereafter never more the same, but each strangely fertilized towards the future? Is it this that explains the extraordinary ecstasy which men experience on the battlefield, even amid all the horrors—an ecstasy so great that it calls them again and again to return? "Have you noticed," says one of our War correspondents,[1] "how many of our colonels fall? Do you know why? It is for five minutes of *life*. It is for the joy of riding, when the charge sounds, at the crest of a wave of men."

Is it this that explains the curious fact that Wars—notwithstanding all their bitterness and brutishness—do not infrequently lead to strange amalgamations and generations? The spreading of the seeds of Greek culture over the then known world by Alexander's conquests, or the fertilizing of Europe with the germs of republican and

[1] H. M. Tomlinson, in the *Daily News*.

revolutionary ideas by the armies of Napoleon, or the immense reaction on the mediæval Christian nations caused by the Crusades, are commonplaces of history; and who—to come to quite modern times—could have foreseen that the Boer War would end in the present positive alliance between the Dutch and English in South Africa, or that the Russo-Japanese conflict would so profoundly modify the ideas and outlook of the two peoples concerned?

In making these remarks I do not for a moment say that the gains resulting from War are worth the suffering caused by it, or that the gains are *not* worth the suffering. The whole subject is too vast and obscure for one to venture to dogmatize on it. I only say that if we are to find any order and law (as we must inevitably *try* to do) in these convulsions of peoples, these tempests of human history, it is probably in the direction that I have indicated.

Of course we need not leave out of sight the ordinary theory and explanation, that wars are simply a part of the general struggle for existence—culminating explosions of hatred and mutual destruction between peoples who are competing with each other for the means of subsistence. That there is something in this view one can hardly deny; and it is one which I have already touched upon. Still, I cannot help thinking that there is something even deeper—something that connects War with the amatory instinct; and that this probably is to be found in the direction of a physiological impact and fusion between the two (or more) peoples concerned, which fertilizes and regenerates them, and is perhaps as necessary in the life of Nations as the fusion of cells is in the life of Protozoa, or the phenomena of sex in the evolution of Man.

And while the Nations fight, the little mortals who represent them have only the faintest idea of what is really going on, of what the warfare means. They *feel* the sweep of immense passions; ecstasies and horrors convulse and dislocate their minds; but they do not, cannot, understand. And the dear creatures in the trenches and the firing-lines give their lives—equally beautiful, equally justified, on both sides: fascinated, rapt, beyond and beside themselves, as foes hating each other with a deadly hatred ; seized with hideous, furious, nerve-racking passions ; performing heroic, magnificent deeds, suffering untold, indescribable wounds and pains, and lying finally side by side (as not unfrequently happens) on the deserted battlefield, reconciled and redeemed and clasping hands of amity even in death.

XIV

THE OVER-POPULATION SCARE

SOME cheerful and rather innocent people insist that because of the over-population difficulty wars must go on for ever. The population of the world, they say—or at any rate of the civilized countries—is constantly increasing, and if war did not from time to time reduce the numbers there would soon be a deadlock. They seem to think that the only way to solve the problem is for the men to murder each other. This says nothing about the women, who, after all, are the chief instruments of multiplication. It may also be pointed out that even the barbaric method of slaughter is not practicable. Although wars of extermination may have now and then occurred in the past among tribes and small peoples, such wars are not considered decent nowadays; and the numbers killed in modern campaigns—horribly "scientific" and "efficient" as the methods are—is such a small fraction of the population concerned as to have no appreciable result. The population of Germany is about seventy millions, and I suppose the wildest anti-Teuton could hardly hope that *more* than a million Germans will be actually killed in the present conflict—less than 1½ per cent.—a fraction which would probably soon be compensated by the increased uxoriousness of the returning troops.

No, War is no solution for the over-population question. If that question is a difficulty, other means must be employed. We ask therefore: (1) Is it a serious difficulty? (2) If so, what is the remedy?

That over-population is in certain localities a serious difficulty few would deny. China, with her four hundred millions, is probably over-populated; that is, with her present resources in production the population presses against the margin of subsistence and can only just maintain itself. There is evidence to show that in the past the natives of some of the Pacific islands, isolated in the great ocean and unable to migrate to other lands, have suffered from the same trouble. Britain is often said to be over-populated; but here quite other considerations come in. Though it might be pleasant for many reasons to have more land at our immediate command, we cannot fairly say that our population presses against the margin of subsistence, for the simple reason that with our immense powers of industrial production and the enormous wealth here yearly obtained the total, if evenly distributed (anything like as well, for instance, as in China), would yield to every man, woman, and child in the United Kingdom an ample affluence.[1] The *appearance* here of over-population arises from the fact that while the wage-earners actually produce this mass of wealth, two-thirds of it are taken by the employers and employing classes. Great portions, therefore, of the actual producers or producing classes *are* on the margin of subsistence, while the rest of the wealth of the country is absorbed by those trading and dividend-consuming classes of

[1] Militating also against the idea of over-population is the fact that so much of our agricultural land is obviously uncared for and neglected.

whom I have spoken more than once in previous pages. There is over-population certainly, but it is an over-population (as any one may see who walks through the West End of London or the corresponding quarters of any of our large towns) of idlers and futile people, who are a burden to the nation. With our extraordinary industrial system–or want of system–it commonly happens that the abundance of ill-paid or unemployed workers at one end of the social scale, by reducing the rates of wages and so increasing the rates of dividends, actually creates a greater abundance of unemployed rich at the other end; but neither excess points in itself to over-population–only to a diseased state of distribution. What we really ought to aim at creating is a nation in which every one was capable of doing useful or beautiful work of some kind or other and was gladly occupied in doing it. Such a nation would be truly healthy. It would be powerful and productive beyond all our present dreams. But the Western nations of to-day, with their huge burdens of unskilled, ill-grown poor and their huge burden of incompetent, feeble rich–it is a wonder that they survive. They would not survive a decade or two if the Chinese or the Japanese in their numbers were to come into personal and direct competition with them.

If Britain is not really at present over-populated, the same is probably even more true of Germany. For Germany, with a larger and more fertile area in proportion to her population, is safer than we are in the matter of self-support. But again in Germany the outcry of over-population has arisen, and has arisen from the same cause as here–namely, the rise of the commercial system, the division of the nation into extremes of poverty and riches, and the consequent *appearance* of excess population in both directions. And this diseased state of the nation has led to a fever of "expansion" and has been (as already said) one of the chief causes of the present war. As long as the modern nations are such fools as to conduct their industrial affairs in the existing way they will not only be full of strife, disease, and discord in themselves, but they will inevitably quarrel with their neighbours.

All this, however, does not prove that a genuine over-population difficulty may not occur even now in localities, and possibly in some far future time over the whole earth. And it may be just as well to consider these possibilities.

Dismissing War and Disease as solutions—as belonging to barbarous and ignorant ages of human evolution—there remain, perhaps, three rational methods of dealing with the question: (1) the organization and improvement of industrial production on existing lands so far as to allow the support of a larger population; (2) the transport of excess populations to new and undeveloped lands (colonization); (3) the limitation of families.

The first method hardly needs discussion here. Its importance is too obvious. It needs, however, more public discussion in England than it has hitherto received. The second method—operating at present only in a very casual and unsystematic way—ought, one would say, to be very systematically considered and dealt with by the modern States. For a nation to plant out large bodies of colonists on comparatively unoccupied lands, as in Africa or Australia or Canada, in a deliberate and organized fashion, with every facility towards co-operation and success, and yet on the principle of leaving each colonial unit plenty of freedom and autonomy, would not be a very difficult task, nor a very expensive one, considering the end in view. And in such a case there would really be no adequate reason for jealousy between States having colonies in the neighbourhood of each other. If Germany (or any other country) wishes to have a colony in East Africa or West Africa, it is really ridiculous to go to war about such a matter. Any peaceful arrangement would be less expensive; and, as a matter of fact, a flourishing German (or other) colony in the neighbourhood of a British settlement would help to bring prosperity to the latter. The two colonies would benefit each other. It is only *unreasoning jealousy* which prevents people understanding this.

Finally, there is the third method, of the intentional limitation of families. Surely the time has come when blind and unlimited propagation among civilized and self-respect-ing peoples must come to an end. The old text "Blessed is he that hath his quiver full of them" has ceased to have any use or application. Eugenic and healthy conditions of child-rearing and nurture demand small families. The well-to-do and educated do already limit their families; and for the poorer classes to breed and propagate indefinitely is only to play into the hands of the dividend-hunting rich by increasing the supply of cheap labour, while at the same time the general standard of the population becomes more and more degraded. It is indeed a curious question why, in the Press and among the official classes, every effort to spread abroad the knowledge of how in a healthy, humane, and eugenic way to limit the size of the family is discountenanced. Sometimes one thinks that this is done partly in order to encourage that said pullulation of workers which is so favourable to the keeping down of wages; but, of course, ancient reasons of ignorance and religious bias weigh also. In the United States the persecutions of Comstockery are worse than here.

The aborigines of Australia are so ignorant

that they do not even know that conception arises from the meeting of the male and female elements. They think that certain bushes and trees are haunted by the spirits of babies, which leap unawares into the bodies of passing women. It can be imagined what evils and delusions spring from such a theory. We do not want to return to such a period; and yet it would seem that many folk do not want to go forward from our present condition, with all *its* evils and delusions, to something better and more intelligent.

If the nations haven't the sense to be able (if they wish) to limit their families—short of resorting to such methods as War, Cannibalism, the spread of Disease, the exposure of Infants, and the like—one can only conclude that they must go on fighting and preying upon each other (industrially and militarily) till they gain the sense. Mere unbridled and irrational lust may have led to wars of extermination in the past. Love and the sacrament of a true and intimate union may come some day with the era of peace.

XV

THE FRIENDLY AND THE FIGHTING INSTINCTS

January, 1915.

FIGHTING is certainly a deeply ingrained instinct in the human race—the masculine portion. In the long history of human development it has undoubtedly played an important part. It has even (such is the cussedness and contrariety of Nature) helped greatly in the evolution of love and social solidarity. There is no greater bond in early stages between the members of a group or tribe than the consciousness that they have a common enemy.[1] It is also obviously still a great *pleasure* to a very large proportion of our male populations—as, indeed, the fact

[1] And even the hundred and one humane Associations of to-day derive a great part of their enthusiasm and vitality from fighting each other!

of its being the fulfilment of a deep instinct would lead us to expect. It does not follow, however, from these remarks that we expect war in its crudest form to continue for ever. There will come a term to this phase of evolution. Probably the impact and collision between nations—if required for their impregnation and fecundity—will come about in some other way.

If fighting is an ingrained instinct, the sociable or friendly instinct is equally ingrained We may, indeed, suppose it roots deeper. In the midst of warfare maddest foes will turn and embrace each other. In the tale of *Cuchulain of Muirthemne*[1] he (Cuchulain) and Ferdiad fought for three days on end, yet at the close of each day kissed each other affectionately; and in the present war there are hundreds of stories already in circulation of acts of grace and tenderness between enemies, as well as the quaintest quips and jokes and demonstrations of sociability between men in opposing trenches who "ought" to have been slaying each other. In the Russo-Japanese War

[1] Put into English by Lady Gregory. (John Murray, 6s. net.)

during the winter, when military movement was not easy, and the enemy lines in some cases were very near each other, the men, Russians and Japanese, played games together as a convenient and pleasant way of passing the time, and not unfrequently took to snowballing each other.

A friend of mine, who was in that war, told me the following story. The Japanese troops were attacking one of the forts near Port Arthur with their usual desperate valour. They cut zig-zag trenches up the hillside, and finally stormed and took a Russian trench close under the guns of the fort. The Russians fled, leaving their dead and wounded behind. After the *mêlee,* when night fell, five Japanese found themselves in that particular trench with seven Russians —all pretty badly wounded—with many others of course dead. The riflemen in the fort were in such a nervous state, that at the slightest movement in the trench they fired, regardless of whom they might hit. The whole party remained quiet during the night and most of the next day. They were suffering from wounds, and without food or water, but they dared not move; they managed, however, to converse with each other a little—especially through the Japanese lieutenant, who knew a little Russian. On the second night the fever for water became severe. One of the less wounded Russians volunteered to go and fetch some. He raised himself from the ground, stood up in the darkness, but was discerned from the fort, and shot. A second Russian did the same and was shot. A Japanese did likewise. Then the rest lay quiet again. Finally, the darkness having increased and the thirst and the wounds being intolerable, the Japanese lieutenant, who had been wounded in the legs and could not move about, said that if one of the remaining Russians would take him on his back he would guide the whole party into a place of safety in the Japanese lines. So they did. The Russian soldier crawled on his belly with the Japanese officer lying on his back, and the others followed, keeping close to the ground. They reached the Japanese quarters, and were immediately looked after and cared for. A few days afterwards the five Russians came on board the transport on which my friend was engineer. They were being taken as prisoners to Japan; but the Japanese crew could not do enough for them in the way of tea and cigarettes and dressing their wounds, and they made quite a jolly party all together on deck. The Japanese officer was also on board, and he told my friend the story.

Gallantry towards the enemy has figured largely in the history of War—sometimes as an individual impulse, sometimes as a recognized instruction. European records afford us plenty of examples. The Chinese, always great sticklers for politeness, used to insist in early times that a warrior should not take advantage of his enemy when the latter had emptied his quiver, but wait for him to pick up his arrows before going on with the fight. And in one tale of old Japan, when one Daimio was besieging another, the besieged party, having run short of ammunition, requested a truce in order to fetch some more—which the besiegers courteously granted!

The British officer who the other day picked up a wounded German soldier and carried him across into the German lines, acted in quite the same spirit. He saw that the man had been left accidentally when the Germans were clearing away their wounded; and quite simply he walked forward with the object of restoring him. But it cost him his life; for the Germans, not at first perceiving his intention, fired and hit him in two or three places. Nevertheless he lifted the man and succeeded in bearing him to the German trench. The firing of course ceased, and the German colonel saluted and thanked the officer, and pinned a ribbon to his coat. He returned to the British lines, but died shortly after of the wounds received.

"Ils sont superbes, ces braves!" said a French soldier in hospital to Mrs. Haden Guest, indicating the German wounded also there. And a dying German whispered to her: "I would never have fought against the French and English had I known how kind they were. I was told that I was only going on manœuvres!"[1]

The French are generous in the recognition of bravery. A small company rushed a Prussian battery in the neighbourhood of the

[1] From *T. P.'s Weekly*, November 7, 1914.

Aisne and put all the gunners out of action, except one who fought gamely to the last and would not give in till he was fairly surrounded and made prisoner. "*Tu es chic, tu—tu es bien chic,*" shouted the *piou-pious* with one accord, and shook him cordially by the hand as they led him away.

How preposterous do such stories as these make warfare appear!—and others, such as the two opposing forces tacitly agreeing to fetch water at the evening hour from an intervening stream without molestation on either side; or the two parties using an old mill as a post-office, by means of which letters could pass between France and Germany in defiance of all decent war-regulations! How they illustrate the absolutely instinctive and necessary tendency of the natural man (notwithstanding occasional bouts of fury) to aid his fellow and fall into some sort of understanding with him! Finally the fraternizations last Christmas between the opposing lines in Northern France almost threatened at one time to dissolve all the proprieties of official warfare. If they had spread a little farther and lasted a little longer, who knows what might have happened? High politics might have been utterly confounded, and the elaborate schemes of statesmen on both sides entirely frustrated. Headquarters had, through the officers, to interfere and all such demonstrations of amity to be for the future forbidden. Could anything more clearly show the beating of the great heart of Man beneath the thickly overlying husks of class and class-government? When, oh! when indeed, will the real human creature emerge from its age-long chrysalis?

XVI

NEVER AGAIN!

LIKE a great cry these words to-day rise from the lips of the nations—"Never Again!" Never before certainly have such enormous masses of human beings been locked in deadly grip with each other over the earth, and never before, equally certainly, has their warfare been so horrible in its deliberate preparation, so hideous, so ghastly in its after-effects, as to-day. The nations stand round paralysed with disgust and despair, almost unable to articulate; and when they do find voice it is with the words above written.

How are we to give effect to the cry? Must we not call upon the Workers of all countries—those who are the least responsible for the inception of wars, and yet who suffer most by them, who bear the brunt of the wounds, the slaughter, the disease, and the misery which are a necessary part of them—to rise up and forbid them for ever from the earth? Let us do so! For though few may follow and join with us to-day, yet to-morrow and every day in the future, and every year, as the mass-peoples come into their own, and to the knowledge of what they are and what they desire to be, those numbers will increase, till the cry itself is no longer a mere cry but an accomplished fact.

It is a hopeful sign that not only among bewildered onlookers and outsiders but among the soldiers themselves (of the more civilized countries) this cry is being taken up. Who, indeed, should know better than they what they are talking about? The same words are on the lips at this moment of thousands and thousands of French and English and German soldiers,[1] and in no faint-hearted or evasive sense, but with the

[1] See "A War-Note for Democrats," by H. M. Tomlinson (*English Review*, December, 1914). "This war was bound to come, and we've got to finish it proper. No more of this bloody rot for the kids, an' chance it."

conviction and indignation of experience. We may hope they will not be forgotten this time when the war is over.

The truth is that not only was this particular war "bound to come," but (among the civilized peoples) the refusal of war is also bound to come. Two great developments are leading to this result. On the one hand, the soldiers themselves, the fighters, are as a class becoming infinitely more sensitive, more intelligent, more capable of humane feeling, less stupidly "patriotic" and prejudiced against their enemies than were the soldiers of a century ago–say, of the time of Wellington; on the other hand, the horrors, the hideousness, the folly, and the waste of war are infinitely greater. It is inevitable that these two contradictory movements, mounting up on opposite sides, must at last clash. The rising conscience of Humanity must in the end say to the War-fiend, "Get thee behind me, Satan!" Never before have there passed over the fields of Europe armies so intelligent, so trained, so observant, so sensitive as those to-day of Belgium, France, England, and Germany. Some day or other they will return to their homes; but when they do it will be with a tale that will give to the Western world an understanding of what war means, such as it never had before.

All the same, if the word *is* to be "Never Again!" it must come through the masses themselves (from whom the fighters are mainly drawn); it must be through them that this consummation must be realized. It must be through the banding together and determined and combined effort of the Unions, local, national, and international, and through the weight of the workers' influence in all their associations and in all countries. To put much reliance in this matter upon the "classes" is rash; for though just now the latter are sentimentalizing freely over the subject—having got into nearer touch with it than ever before—yet when all is settled down, and the day arrives once more that *their* interests point to war, it is only too likely that they (or the majority of them) will not hesitate to sacrifice the masses—unless, indeed, the power to do so has already departed from them.

And it is no good for *us* to sentimentalize on the subject. We must not blink facts.

And the fact is that " it's a long way " to *Never Again* The *causes* of War must be destroyed first; and, as I have more than once tried to make clear, the causes ramify through our midst; they are like the roots, pervading the body politic, of some fell disease whose outbreak on the surface shocks and affrights us. To dislodge and extirpate these roots is a long business. But there is this consolation about it—that it is a business which we can all of us begin at once, in our own lives!

Probably wars will still for many a century continue, though less frequent we hope. And if the people themselves *want* to fight, and must fight, who is to say them Nay? In such case we need not be overmuch troubled. There are many things worse than fighting; and there are many wounds and injuries which people inflict on each other worse than bodily wounds and injuries—only they are not so plain to see. But I certainly would say—as indeed the peasant says in every land—" Let those who begin the quarrel do the fighting "; and let those who have to do the fighting and bear the brunt of it (including the women) decide whether there *shall* be fighting or not. To leave the dread arbitrament of War in the hands of private groups and cliques who, for their own ends and interests, are willing to see the widespread slaughter of their fellow-countrymen and the ruin of innumerable homes is hateful beyond words.

XVII

THE TREE OF LIFE

February, 1915.

FINALLY, and looking back on all we have said, and especially on the Christmas scenes and celebrations between the trenches in this war and the many similar fraternizations of the rank and file of opposing armies in former wars, one realizes the monstrosity and absurdity of the present conflict—its anachronism and out-of-dateness in the existing age of human thought and feeling.

The whole European situation resembles a game of marbles played by schoolboys. It is not much more dignified than that. Each boy tries on the quiet to appropriate some of the marbles out of another boy's bag. From time to time, in consequence, furious scrimmages arise—generally between two boys—the others looking on and laughing, knowing well that they themselves are guilty of the same tricks. Presently, in the fortunes of the game, one boy—a little more blundering or a little less disguised than the others—lays himself open to the accusations of the whole crew. They all fall upon him, and give him a good drubbing; and even some of them say they are punishing him *for his good*! When shall we make an end, once for all, of this murderous nonsense?

However our Tommy Atkinses have been worked up to fighting point by fears for the safety of old England, or by indignation at atrocities actually observed or distantly reported; however the German soldiers have been affected by similar fears and indignations, or the French the same; however the political coil has been engineered (as engineered in such cases it always is), and whatever inducements of pay or patriotism have been put in operation and sentiments circulated by the Press—one thing remains perfectly certain: that left to themselves these men would never have quarrelled, never have attacked each other. One thing is perfectly certain: that such a war as the present is the result of the activity of governing cliques and classes in the various nations, acting through what are called "Diplomatic" channels, for the most part in secret and unbeknown to their respective mass-peoples, and for motives best known to themselves.

One would not venture to say that *all* wars are so engineered, for there certainly are occasionally wars which are the spontaneous expression of two nations' natural hostility and hatred; but these are rare, very rare, and the war in which we are concerned at present is certainly not one of them. Also one would not venture to say that though in the present affair the actuating motives have been of class origin, and have been worked through secret channels, the motives so put in action have all been base and mean. That would be going too far. Some of the motives may have been high-minded and generous, some may have been mean, and others may have been mean and yet *unconsciously* so. But certainly when one looks at the conditions of public and political life, and the arrangements and concatenations by which influence there is exerted and secured, and sees (as one must) the pretty bad corruption which pervades the various parties in all the modern States—the commercial briberies, the lies of the Press, the poses and prevarications of Diplomats and Ministers—one cannot but realize the great probability that the private advantage of individuals or classes has been (in the present case) a prevailing instigation. The fact that in Britain two influential and honourable Cabinet Ministers resigned at once on the declaration of war (a fact upon which the Press has been curiously silent) cannot but "give one to think." One cannot but realize that the fighting men in all these nations are the pawns and counters of a game which is being played for the benefit—or supposed benefit—of certain classes; that public opinion is a huge millstream which has to be engineered; that the Press is a channel for its direction, and Money the secret power which commands the situation.

The fact is sad, but it must be faced. And the facing of it leads inevitably to the question, "How, then, can Healing ever come?" If (it will be said) the origin of wars is in the diseased condition of the nations, what prospect is there of their ever ceasing? And one sees at once that the prospect is not immediate. One sees at once that Peace Societies and Nobel Prizes and Hague Tribunals and reforms of the Diplomatic Service and democratic control of Foreign Secretaries and Quaker and Tolstoyan preachments–though all these things may be good in their way—will never bring us swiftly to the realization of peace. The roots of the Tree of Life lie deeper.

We have seen it a dozen times in the foregoing pages. Only when the nations cease to be diseased in themselves will they cease fighting with each other. And the disease of the modern nations is the disease of disunity —not, as I have already said, the mere existence of variety of occupation and habit, for that is perfectly natural and healthy, but the disease by which one class preys upon another and upon the nation–the disease of parasitism and selfish domination. The health of a people consists in that people's real *unity*, the organic life by which each section contributes freely and generously to the welfare of the whole, identifies itself with that welfare, and holds it a dishonour to snatch for itself the life which should belong to all. A nation which realized *that* kind of life would be powerful and healthy beyond words; it would not only be splendidly glad and prosperous and unassailable in itself, but it would inevitably infect all other nations with whom it had dealings with the same principle. Having the Tree of Life well rooted within its own garden, its leaves and fruit and all its acts and expressions would be for the healing of the peoples around. But a nation divided against itself by parasitic and self-exalting cliques and sections could never stand. It could never be healthy. No armaments nor ingenuity of science and organization could save it, and even though the form of its institutions were democratic, if the reality of Democracy were not there, its peace crusades and prizes and sentimental Conferences and Christianities would be of little avail.

At this juncture, then, all over Europe, when the classes are failing us and by their underhand machinations continually embroiling one nation with another, it is above all necessary that the mass-peoples should move and insist upon the representation of their great unitary and communal life and interests. It is high time that they should open their eyes and see with clear vision what is going on over their heads, and more than high time that they should refuse to take part in the Quarrels of those who (professionally) live upon their labour. It is indeed astonishing that the awakening has been so long in coming; but surely it cannot be greatly delayed now. Underneath all the ambitions of certain individuals and groups; underneath all the greed and chicanery of others; underneath the widespread ignorance, mother of prejudice, which sunders folk of different race or colour—deep down the human heart beats practically the same in all lands, drawing us little mortals together.

Strangely enough—and yet not strangely—it beats strongest and clearest often in the simplest, the least sophisticated. Those who live nearest the truth of their own hearts are nearest to the hearts of others. Those who have known the realities of the world, and what Life is close to the earth—they are the same in all lands—they have at least the key to the understanding of each other. The old needs of life, its destinies and fatalities, its sorrows and joys, its exaltations and depressions—these are the same everywhere; and to the manual workers—the peasant, the labourer, the sailor, the mechanic—the world-old trades, pursuits, crafts, and callings with which they are so familiar supply a kind of freemasonry which ensures them even among strangers a kindly welcome and an easy admittance. If you want to travel in foreign lands, you will find that to be skilled in one or two manual trades is better than a high official passport.

Among such people there is no natural hatred of each other. Despite all the foam and fury of the Press over the present war, I doubt whether there is any really violent feeling of the working masses on either side between England and Germany. There certainly is no great amount in England, either among the countryfolk or the town artisans and mechanics; and if there be much in Germany (which is quite doubtful) it is fairly obviously due to the *animus* which has been aroused and the *virus* which has been propagated by political and social schemers.

We have had enough of Hatred and

Jealousy. For a century now commercial rivalry and competition, the perfectionment of the engines of war, and the science of destruction have sufficiently occupied the nations–with results only of disaster and distress and ruin to all concerned. To-day surely another epoch opens before us–an epoch of intelligent helpfulness and fraternity, an epoch even of the simplest common sense. We have rejoiced to tread and trample the other peoples underfoot, to malign and traduce them, to single out and magnify their defects, to boast ourselves over them. And acting thus we have but made the more enemies. Now surely comes an era of recognition and understanding, and with it the glad assurance that we have friends in all the ends of the earth.

We–and I speak of the European nations generally–have talked loudly of our own glory; but have we welcomed and acclaimed the glory and beauty of the other peoples and races around us—among whom it is our privilege to dwell? We have boasted to love each our own country, but have we cared at all for the other countries too? Verily I suspect that it is because we have *not* truly loved our own countries, but have betrayed them for private profit, that we have thought fit to hate our neighbours and ill-use them for our profit too.

What a wonderful old globe this is, with its jewelled constellations of humanity! Alfred Russel Wallace, in his *Travels on the Amazon* (1853, ch. xvii), says: "I do not remember a single circumstance in my travels so striking and so new, or that so well fulfilled all previous expectation, as my first view of the real uncivilized inhabitants of the river Uaupes. . . . I felt that I was as much in the midst of something new and startling, as if I had been instantaneously transported to a distant and unknown country." He then speaks of the "quiet, good-natured, inoffensive" character of these copper-coloured natives, and of their quickness of hand and skill, and continues: "Their figures are generally superb; and I have never felt so much pleasure in gazing at the finest statue as at these living illustrations of the beauty of the human form." Elsewhere he says[1]: "Their whole aspect

[1] *My Life*, vol ii, p. 288.

and manner were different [from the semi-civilized Indians] ; they walked with the free step of the independent forest-dweller . . . original and self-sustaining as the wild animals of the forest . . . living their own lives in their own way, as they had done for countless generations before America was discovered. The true denizen of the Amazonian forests, like the forest itself, is unique and not to be forgotten."

Not long ago I was talking to a shrewd, vigorous old English lady who had spent some forty years of her life among the Kafirs in South Africa and knew them intimately. She said (not knowing anything about *my* feelings): "Ah! you British think a great deal about yourselves. You think you are the finest race on earth; but I tell you the Kafirs are finer. They are splendid. Whether for their physical attributes, or their mental, or for their qualities of soul, I sometimes think *they* are the finest people in the world." Whether the old lady was right (and one has heard others say much the same), or whether she was carried away by her enthusiasm, the fact remains that here is a people *capable* of exciting such enthusiasm, and certainly capable of exciting much admiration among all who know them well.

Read the accounts of the Polynesian peoples at an early period—before commerce and the missionaries had come among them —as given in the pages of Captain Cook, of Herman Melville, or even as adumbrated in their past life in the writings of R. L. Stevenson—what a picture of health and gaiety and beauty! Surely never was there a more charming and happy folk—even if long-pig did occasionally in their feasts alternate with wild-pig.

And yet how strange that the white man, with all his science and all his so-called Christianity, has only come among these three peoples mentioned (and how many more?) to destroy and defile them—to flog the mild and innocent native of the Amazons to death for greed of his rubber; to rob the Kafir of his free wild lands and blast his life with drink and slavery in the diamond mines; to degrade and exterminate the Pacific islanders with all the vices and diseases of "civilization"!

Think of the Chinese—that extraordinary

people coming down from the remotest ages of history, with their habits and institutions apparently but little changed—so kindly, so "all there," so bent on making the best of this world. "At the first sight of these ugly, cheery, vigorous people I loved them. Their gaiety, as of children, their friendliness, their profound humanity, struck me from the first and remained with me to the last." [1] And the verdict of all who know the people well–in the interior of the country of course–is the same. Think of the Japanese with their slight and simple, but exceedingly artistic and exceedingly heroic type of civilization.

Or, again, of the East Indian peoples, so unfitted as a rule for making the best of this world, so passive, dreamy, subtle, unpractical, and yet with their marvellous spiritual gift, their intuition (also since the dawn of history) and conviction of another plane of being than that in which we mostly move, and their occasional power of distinctly sensing that plane and acting on its

[1] G. Lowes Dickinson, *Civilizations of India, China, and Japan*, p. 43. See also Eugene Simon, *La Citè Chinoise*, passim.

indications. Think of their ancient religious philosophy—their doctrine of world-unity—absolutely foundational and inexpugnable, the corner-stone of all metaphysics, science, and politics, and of the latest most modern democracy; and still realized and believed in in India as nowhere else in the world.

Think of the gentle Buddhistic Burmese, the active, social Malays, the hard-featured, hard-lived Thibetans and Mongolians. Think of the Arabian and Moorish and Berber races, who, once the masters of the science and comforts of civilization, of their own accord (but in accordance also with their religion) abandoned the worship of all these idols and returned to the Biblical simplicity of four thousand years ago—having realized that they already possessed something better, namely, the glory of the sky and the earth, the sun and the desert sands, and the freedom of love and adventure. How strange, and yet how natural, that sundered only by a narrow strip of sea they even now should look back upon all the laborious, feverish, and overcrowded wealth of Europe and *seeing the cost thereof* should feel for it only contempt! For that, indeed, is actually for the most part the case—though not of course without exceptions among certain sections of the population.

Or again, the millions and millions of Great and Little Russian peasants. Big-framed, big-hearted, patient, friendly, with a great natural gift for association and co-operation, peacefully minded and profoundly religious; yet superstitious, and capable of rising at any moment *en masse* to the call of a great crusade or "holy war"; it might seem that they hold all Western Europe in the hollow of their hands. Indeed they constitute not only a hope and promise of deliverance to our modern world, but also a considerable danger. All depends on how we dispose ourselves towards them. Should the nations of Western Europe rouse their hatred by chicanery and mean treatment the result might be fatal. If their flood once began to move, no battle array of armaments would be of any use–any more than a revolver against a rising tide—the flood would flow round and over us. But if on the other hand we could really reach the heart of this great people, if we could treat them really generously and with understanding, we should create a response there, and a recognition, which would remove all risk to ourselves, and possibly help to free Russia from the great burden of political servitude and ignorance which has so long oppressed her peasantry.

Or think of the Servians—that hospitable people, good lovers and good haters, with their ancient, almost prehistoric, system of family communities surviving down to modern days, and blossoming out in a perfect genius for co-operative agriculture and Raffeisen banks!

Or the Finns, the Swedes, the Norwegians, and the Danes (if I may class these together); what a clear, clean-minded, healthy people are these, so direct in their touch on Nature and the human instincts, so democratic, bold, and progressive in their social organizations—what a privilege to have them as our near neighbours and relatives! Or the Germans, in many ways resembling the last mentioned group, only richer and more varied in their culture and racial characteristics! Or the Dutch, so well-based and broad-seated both in body and mind, with their ample bowels of compassion and their well-equipped brains, so full of tenderness and of sturdy commonsense, what a gift has been theirs to Europe, what a legacy of artistic treasure and of heroic record! Or the Spanish with their beautiful and dignified women, or the French with their fine logical and artistic sense, or the Hungarians, Greeks, and Italians!

Have we nothing to do but to prepare engines of death and of slaughter against all these peoples? Is our main idea of relation to them one of domination and profit? Have we no use for them but to gain their riches, and in exchange to lose our own souls? Or shall we, like the Prussians, seek to "impose" our own standards of so-called culture on them, and trim their infinite variety and grace to one sorry pattern? These are all in their diverse glory and beauty as leaves of the one great Tree whose branches spread over the earth. Whoever understands this, and penetrating to the great heart beneath, recognizes the same original life in them all, will possess the secret of salvation; whatever nation first casts aside the filthy rags of its own self-righteousness and the defiling and sordid garment of mercenary gain, and accepts the others frankly as its brother and sister nations, all of one family–that nation will become the Healer and Redeemer of the World.

It is interesting to find that, according to the Book of Revelation, the tree of which we have been speaking grows with its roots "in the pure river of the water of Life, which proceeds from the throne of God and the Lamb." What exactly the author of the book meant by this passage has been much debated. It is clear that there is here a veiled allusion to the Zodiac–that mysterious belt of constellations which runs like a river round the whole starry heavens, and rises in the constellation of the Ram or He-lamb–but to debate *that* question now would be unprofitable, even were one fully competent to do so. More to the point is it to see that this remarkable simile has an inner sense applicable to mankind, and so far independent of any allusion to the Zodiac. This Tree that is for the healing of the nations has its roots in the pure water of Life which flows from the great Throne. We have seen in an early chapter where the roots of Strife between the nations are to be sought for, and whence they draw their nourishment. They are to be found in the very muddy waters of domination and selfishness and greed. But the roots of the Tree of Healing are in the pure waters of Life. Right down below all the folly and meanness which clouds men's souls flows the universal Life pure from its original source. The longer you live, the more clearly and certainly you will perceive it. In the eyes of the men and women around you you will perceive it, and in the eyes of the children—aye, and even of the animals. Unclean, no doubt, will the surface be—muddied with meannesses and self-motives; and among those classes and currents of people who chiefly delight to dwell in the midst of such things (who dwell in the floating mire of malice and envy and self-assertion and avarice and conceit and deceit and domination and other such refuse), the waters will be foul indeed; but below these classes, among the simple, comparatively unselfconscious types of humanity who everywhere represent the universal life (without, in a sense, being aware of it), and again, above them, among those whose spirits have passed "in compassion and determination around the whole earth and found only equals and lovers," the water flows pure and free. These two groups—between them forming far the largest and most important mass of human kind—are those whose influence and tendency is toward peace and amity. It is only the scurrying, avaricious, fever-stricken, and, for all their wealth, poverty-stricken classes and cliques of the civilization-period who are the sources of discord and strife—and they only for a time. In the end it will be found that by every river and stream and tiny brook over the whole earth grows the invincible Tree of Life, whose roots are deep in the human heart, and whose leaves are for the healing of the Nations.

APPENDIX

[THE following extracts, mostly from contemporaneous sources, are gathered together in an Appendix with the object of throwing side-lights, *often from opposing points of view*, on the questions raised in the text.]

APPENDIX

A New and Better Peace.

"If we now destroy the German national idol, it must not be to set up an idol of our own in its place. There will be ruin enough after the war to repair, and a heavy task for all the nations in repairing it; but if they have learned then that peace is not a disguised war but a state of being in which men and nations alike pursue their own ideas of excellence without rivalry, then we shall know that the irrevocable dead have not died in vain.—*"Times" Literary Supplement, September* 17, 1914.

The Change from the Germany of Kant and Goethe and Schubert to the Germany of To-day—and the Delusion of Imperialism.

"What, then, has wrought this wonderful change in a people so closely allied to ourselves, whose race is so similar that their children in the hotels of France and Italy are mistaken for British children? The human raw material is the same, and until half a century ago gave results which won our respect and admiration. What is this change of the last half-century which from the same material gives results so different? There can be only one answer. The old Germany was a Germany of small, self-governing States, of small political power; the new Germany is a 'great' Germany, with a new ideal and spirit which comes of victory and military and political power, of the reshaping of political and social institutions which the retention of conquered territory demands, its militarization, regimentation, centralization, and unchallenged authority; the cultivation of the spirit of domination, the desire to justify and to frame a philosophy to buttress it. Some one has spoken of the war which made 'Germany great and Germans small.' . . ."

". . . So in our day, it is not the German national faith, the *Deutschtum*, the belief that the German national ideal is best for the German—it is not that belief that is a danger to Europe. It is a belief that that German national ideal is the best for all other people, and that the Germans have a right to impose it by the force of their armies. It is that belief alone which can be destroyed by armies. We must show that we do not intend to be brought under German rule, or have German ideals imposed upon us, and having demonstrated that, the Allies must show that they in their turn have no intention of imposing their ideals or their rule or their dominance upon German peoples. The Allies must show after this war that they do not desire to be the masters of the German peoples or States, but their partners and associates in a Europe which none shall dominate, but which all shall share."—*From "Shall this War End German Militarism?" by Norman Angell.*

German Public Opinion in 1913 with Regard to the Impending War.

The Report on this subject given in the French Yellow Book (Section 5) throws much light on the attitude of the various classes in Germany. In favour of peace (it says) are "the large mass of workmen, artisans, and peasants, who are peaceful by instinct"; a considerable number of non-military nobility, and of "manufacturers, merchants, and financiers of minor importance, to whom even a victorious war would bring bankruptcy"; also a vast number of those who are continually in a state of "suppressed revolt against Prussian policy," like the "Government and ruling classes of the great southern States, Saxony, Bavaria, Wurtemburg," and so forth.

On the other hand, in favour of war are the great, mainly Prussian, war party, consisting of the military aristocracy and nobility "who see with terror the democratization of Germany and the growing force of the Socialist party"; "others who consider war as necessary for economic reasons found in over-population and over-production, the need of markets and outlets"; the great *bourgeoisie*, "which also has its reasons of a social nature—the upper middle class being no less affected than the nobility by the democratization of Germany . . . and, finally, the gun and armour-plate manufacturers, the great merchants who clamour for greater markets, and the bankers who speculate on the Golden Age and the indemnity of war. These, too, think that war would be good business."

The whole paper is too long for extensive citation here, but is well worth reading.

Political Ignorance in Germany.

"On Tuesday last at the Union Society Mr. Dudley Ward, late Berlin correspondent of the *Daily Chronicle* and other English papers, and Fellow of St. John's College, dealt with 'The War from the German Point of View.' Mr. Ward's profound knowledge of Germany, especially since 1911, and his obvious attempt to review recent events with impartiality, was a revelation to Cambridge, and a very large audience showed its enthusiastic appreciation of his ability and his frankness.

"Mr. Ward emphasized particularly the *astonishing political ignorance* of the German people as a whole, an ignorance quite unintelligible to any one unacquainted with their Press and their political institutions. Public opinion, as he said, counts for little in Germany, and the Government can generally guide it into any direction it may please, and this fact is essential to the understanding of the events—diplomatic events—which led to the declaration of war."—*From the "Cambridge Magazine," December* 5, 1914.

"One of the political phenomena of America has always been the indifference of the German to active participation in politics. Efforts to persuade him to organize with any political party have never succeeded except in isolated cases. The German-American has been regarded as an independent politically. Until Europe's conflict raised concealed characteristics to the surface the German-American's indifference to politics had not been looked upon as a serious matter."—*From article by Mr. John Herbert in the London "Daily News," December,* 1914.

Germany's Purpose.

According to Herr Maximilien Harden's article in "Die Zukunft," as reproduced in the "New York Times," December, 1914.

"Not as weak-willed blunderers have we undertaken the fearful risk of this war. We wanted it. Because we had to wish it and could wish it. May the Teuton devil throttle those whiners whose pleas for excuses make us ludicrous in these hours of lofty experience. We do not stand, and shall not place ourselves, before the Court of Europe. Our power shall create new law in Europe. Germany strikes. If it conquers new realms for its genius, the priesthood of all the gods will sing songs of praise to the good war.

"We are at the beginning of a war the development and duration of which are incalculable, and in which up to date no foe has been brought to his knees. We wage the war in order to free enslaved peoples, and thereafter to comfort ourselves with the unselfish and useless consciousness of our own righteousness. We wage it from the lofty point of view and with the conviction that Germany, as a result of her achievements and in proportion to them, is justified in asking, and must obtain, wider room on earth for development and for working out the possibilities that are in her."

England's Perfidy.

From the Manifesto of Professors Haeckel and Eucken, September, 1914.

"What is happening to-day surpasses every instance from the past; this last example will be permanently characterized in the annals of the world as the *indelible shame of England.* Great Britain is fighting for a Slavic, semi-Asiatic Power *against Teutonism;* she is fighting, not only in the ranks of barbarism but also on the side of *wrong and injustice,* for let it not be forgotten that Russia began the war, because she refused to permit adequate expiation for a miserable assassination; but the blame for extending the limits of the present conflict to the proportions of a world-war, through which the sum of human culture is threatened, rests upon England.

"And the reason for all this? Because England was *envious* of Germany's greatness, because she was bound to hinder further expansion of the German sphere at any cost! There cannot be the least doubt that England was determined from the start to break in upon Germany's great conflict for *national existence,* to cast as many stones as possible in Germany's path, and to block her every effort toward adequate expansion. England lay in wait until the favourable opportunity for inflicting a lasting injury upon Germany should come, and promptly seized upon *the unavoidable German invasion of Belgian territory* as a pretext for draping her own brutal national egotism in a mantle of decency.

"*Or is there in the whole world a person so simple as to believe that England would have declared war upon France, had the latter Power invaded Belgium?* In that event, England would have shed hypocritical tears over the necessary violation of international law, while concealing a laughing face behind the mask. The most repulsive thing in the whole business is this hypocritical Pharisaism; it merits only contempt.

"History shows that such sentiments as these, far from guiding nations upward, lead them along the downward path. But we of this present time have fixed our faith firm as a rock upon our righteous cause, and upon the superior power and the inflexible will for victory that abide in the German nation. Nevertheless the deplorable fact remains, that the boundless egotism already mentioned has for that span of the future discernible to us destroyed the collaboration of the two nations which was so full of promise for the intellectual uplift of humanity. But the other party has willed it so. Upon England alone rests the monstrous guilt and the responsibility in the eye of world-history."

"ERNST HAECKEL.
"RUDOLF EUCKEN."

FROM THE MANIFESTO OF PROFESSOR EUCKEN.

"Let us hope that our German weapons will show the Englishmen that they were entirely wrong in their reckoning; but first let us point out the wide discrepancy between their motives and ours.

"With them it is self-seeking, envy, calculation; with us the conviction that we are fighting for the holiest possessions of our people, for right and justice."

Nietzsche on Disarmament.

The following extract from *Nietzsche* may be worth quoting as presenting one aspect of his many-sided thought:—

"Perhaps a memorable day will come when a nation renowned in wars and victories, distinguished by the highest development of military order and intelligence, and accustomed to make the heaviest sacrifices for these objects, will voluntarily exclaim, 'We will break our swords,' and will destroy its whole military system, lock, stock, and barrel. To make ourselves defenceless (after having been most strongly defended), from loftiness of sentiment, is the means towards genuine peace. . . . The so-called armed peace that prevails at present in all countries is a sign of a bellicose disposition, that trusts neither itself nor its neighbour, and, partly from hate partly from fear, refuses to lay down its weapons. Better to perish than to hate and fear; and twice better to perish than to make oneself hated and feared."—*From "Human all too Human," vol. ii. (translated by P. V. Colm,* 1911).

The Effect of Disarmament.

"Just as the growth of armaments increases the common danger, so a policy of reduction would have the opposite effect, and were one European country boldly to adopt disarmament it would strengthen incalculably the forces making for peace in all countries. The armaments of European nations are interdependent, and were such a policy pursued by one nation it would be followed, if not by immediate disarmament in other nations, at any rate, by very considerable reductions. It is very easy to underrate the feeling which for some time past has been growing throughout Europe against the colossal waste of armaments. Even in Germany, whose geographical position from a military point of view is weak, the Socialist vote, which is cast strenuously against armaments, has grown at each election until it now represents some 35 per cent. of the total electorate. The great weapon with which reaction has attempted to combat Socialist growth has been an appeal against the 'unpatriotic' opposition to armaments. What effect would this appeal have in face of disarmament abroad? The Socialist party, with its anti-militarist programme, would sweep Germany and compel the Government rapidly to follow suit. Sooner or later the internal pressure of public opinion would force the adoption of a similar policy upon the Government of every civilized country in Europe."—*From "Why Britain Should Disarm," by George Benson (National Labour Press, 1d.).*

The Principle of Nationality.

"Now the war has come, and when it is over let us be careful not to make the same mistake or the same sort of mistake as Germany made when she had France prostrate at her feet in 1870. (Cheers.) Let us, whatever we do, fight for and work towards great and sound principles for the European system. And the first of those principles which we should keep before us is the principle of nationality—that is to say, not the conquest or subjugation of any great community or of any strong race of men, but the setting free of those races which have been subjugated and conquered; and if doubt arises about disputed areas of country we should try to settle their ultimate destination in the reconstruction of Europe which must follow from this war with a fair regard to the wishes and feelings of the people who live in them."—*From the speech of Mr. Churchill, September* 11, 1914, at the London Opera House.

Conscription.

"If we, in a moment of unthinking panic, adopt the advice of our militarists and develop an Army based on universal service, we shall prepare for ourselves the very situation in which Germany finds itself at this moment. However much we may protest that our aims are pacific, and that our Army is intended only for defensive purposes, foreign nations will view it with alarm, and will reflect that, by the help of our Navy, we can land an armed force in any country that has a sea coast. We shall thus incur the risk of a coalition against us. It is said that if we had had a conscript Army, the present war would not have taken place. But it is not realized that a different and far more dangerous war would have been probable, a war in which we should have had no continental Allies, but should have been resisted, as Germany is being resisted, in order to relieve Europe of an intolerable terror. . . .

"In a word, of all the measures open to us to adopt, none is so likely to bring us to disaster as universal military service."—*By Hon. Bertrand Russell (in "The Labour Leader," October* 15, 1914).

H. G. Wells on the Regulation of Armaments and Neutralization of the Sea.

"If there is courage and honesty enough in men, I believe it will be possible to establish a world Council for the regulation of armaments as the natural outcome of this war. First, the trade in armaments must be absolutely killed. And then the next supremely important measure to secure the peace of the world is the neutralization of the sea.

"It will lie in the power of England, France,

Russia, Italy, Japan, and the United States, if Germany and Austria are shattered in this war, to forbid the further building of any more ships of war at all."—*From the "Daily Chronicle," August* 21, 1914.

THE WAR AND DEMOCRACY.

"It will be necessary soon to consider the relations of democracy to the war. The war is a war of nationalities, but it was not made by peoples. Its begetter was a comparatively small band of unscrupulous, blind, and conceited persons, who were clever and persistent enough to demoralize a whole people. In so far as they permitted themselves to be demoralized the people were to blame, but the chief blame lies on the small band. Europe is laid waste, hundreds of thousands of men murdered, and practically every human being in the occidental hemisphere made to suffer, not for the amelioration of a race, but in order to satisfy the idiotic ambitions of a handful. Let not this fact be forgotten. Democracy will not forget it. And foreign policy in the future will not be left in the hands of any autocracy, by whatever specious name the autocracy may call itself. Ruling classes have always said that masses were incapable of understanding foreign policy. The masses understand it now. They understand that in spite of very earnest efforts in various Cabinets, the ruling classes have failed to avert the most terrible disaster in history. The masses will say to themselves, 'At any rate we couldn't have done worse than that.' The masses know that if the war decision had been openly submitted to a representative German chamber, instead of being taken in concealment and amid disgusting chicane, no war would have occurred. It is absolutely certain that the triumph of democracy, and nothing else, will end war as an institution. War will be ended when the Foreign Offices are subjected to popular control. That popular control is coming."—*Arnold Bennett in the "Daily News," October* 15, 1914.

The Future Settlement.

Let us turn, then, from the past to the future and ask, first, what the governmental mind, left to itself, is likely to make of Europe when the war is finished; secondly, what we, on our part, want and mean to make of it. What the diplomatists will make of it is written large on every page of history. Again and again they have "settled" Europe, and always in such a way as to leave roots for the growth of new wars. For always they have settled it from the point of view of States, instead of from the point of view of human life. How one "Power" may be aggrandized and another curtailed, how the spoils may be divided among the victors, how the "balance" may be arranged—these kinds of considerations and these alone have influenced their minds. The desires of peoples, the interests of peoples, that sense of nationality which is as real a thing as the State is fictitious—to all that they have been indifferent. . . .

What can be foreseen with certainty is, that if the peace is to be made by the same men who made the war it will be so made that in another quarter of a century there will be another war on as gigantic a scale. . . .

When this war is over Europe might be settled, then and there, if the peoples so willed it and made their will effective, in such a way that there would never again be a European War. . . .

First, the whole idea of aggrandizing one nation and humiliating another must be set aside. . . . Secondly, in rearranging the boundaries of States, one point, and one only, must be kept in mind : to give to all peoples suffering and protesting under alien rule the right to decide whether they will become an autonomous unit, or will join the political system of some other nation. . . . Let no community be coerced under British rule that wants to be self-governing. We have had the courage, though late, to apply this principle to South Africa and Ireland. There remains our greatest act of courage and wisdom—to apply it to India.—*G. Lowes Dickinson, "The War and the Way Out," pp.* 34 *et seq.*

A War Note for Democrats.

"The truth about the present fighting—well, it cannot be rendered in words significant enough to shock into understanding the people who are looking in the newspapers now for stories of heroism, 'brilliant bayonet charges,' and the rest of the inducements which sell stories of warfare, but tell us nothing about it. Perhaps, indeed, there are no words for it. I doubt whether the sincerest artist, finely sensitive, and with the choicest army of words at his ready and accurate command, could assemble the case. The mind of a witness in France is not stirred; it is stunned. One is speechless before the spectacle of men, not fighting in the way two angry men would fight, but coolly blasting great masses of their opponents to pieces at long range, and out of sight of each other, till a region with its wrecked towns and homesteads is littered with human bowels and fragments. It is possible to value human life too highly, maybe. But what profit, physical, moral, or economic, can be got from draining several nations' best male generative force into the clay, I leave it to worshippers of tribal war-gods of whatever church, and to the military minds, to explain. But unless the democracies of Europe, after settling this business, see to securing such a settlement—whatever the governing classes desire—that this Continental waste can never occur again, then one would have to admit human nature is too stupid and base to be troubled over any longer."—*H. M. Tomlinson, "English Review," December, 1914, p. 75.*

Patriotism!

"It would seem, then, that love of our country can flourish only through the hatred of other countries, and the massacre of those who sacrifice themselves in defence of them. There is in this theory a ferocious absurdity, a Neronian dilettantism which repels me in the very depths of my being. No! Love of my country does not demand that I shall hate and slay those noble and faithful souls who also love their country, but rather that I should honour them, and seek to unite myself with them for our common good. . . .

"You Socialists on both sides claim to be defending liberty against tyranny—French liberty against the Kaiser, Germany liberty against the Tsar. Would you defend one despotism against another? *Unite and make war on both.* There was no reason for war between the Western nations; French, English, and German, we are all brothers, and do not hate one another. The war-preaching Press is envenomed by a minority, a minority vitally interested in maintaining these hatreds; but our peoples, I know, ask for peace and liberty, and that alone."—*From Romain Rolland's pamphlet "Above the Battlefield," Cambridge, 1914.*

No Patriotism in Business!

The following leaderette is from the *Glasgow Evening Citizen* for the 15th of January :—

"In business patriotism does not enter. Insistently the pocket comes first. And if the British consumer of aniline dyes can obtain his raw material more advantageously from the German than from the British producer, he will probably be ready to do so for the greater gain of more economic production in his own business."

Manifesto of the Independent Labour Party.

"We desire neither the aggrandizement of German militarism nor Russian militarism, but the danger is that this war will promote one or the other. Britain has placed herself behind Russia, the most reactionary, corrupt, and oppressive Power in Europe. If Russia is permitted to gratify her territorial ambitions and extend her Cossack rule, civilization and democracy will be gravely imperilled. Is it for this that Britain has drawn the sword?

"To us who are Socialists the workers of Germany and Austria, no less than the workers of France and Russia, are comrades and brothers; in this hour of carnage and eclipse we have friendship and compassion to all victims of militarism. Our nationality and independence, which are dear to us, we are ready to defend, but we cannot rejoice in the organized murder of tens of thousands of workers of other lands who go to kill and be killed at the command of rulers to whom the people are as pawns.

"The People must everywhere resist such territorial aggression and national abasement as will pave the way for fresh wars; and, throughout Europe, the workers must press for frank and honest diplomatic policies, controlled by themselves, for the suppression of militarism and the establishment of the United States of Europe, thereby advancing towards the world's peace. Unless these steps are taken Europe, after the present calamity, will be still more subject to the increasing domination of militarism, and liable to be drenched with blood."

Responsibility rests on the whole Capitalist Class.

"Prussian militarism, as we have shown in previous issues, exists, as all militarism does, to further and protect trade. The furtherance of that trade meant territorial expansion, which in its turn was a menace to Britain and her allies. Thus it is that this war, carefully manœuvred by the diplomats, is being fought to conserve to one set of capitalists their right to exploit the peoples, and to check another set from encroaching upon that right.

"Germany—or rather, the capitalists of Germany, for whom the Kaiser has always been the "Publicity Agent"—has consistently worked toward the objective of challenging the right of Britain to a world-wide Empire. To the German capitalists this war is but the realization of their philosophy, "Might is Right," and, reckless of human life and suffering, a European war is to them the way to vaster fields of exploitation and greater wealth. Their militarism was the machine, and the workers the cogs of the wheels. British capitalists, on the other hand, determined to maintain what they hold, forgetful of how it had been obtained, were thus compelled to take up the cudgels for their own sakes; and here, as in Germany, the workers are the tools used to save their fortunes and conserve their rights."—"*The Voice of Labour,*" *October*, 1914.

"And it is not unlikely that the present bloody catastrophe will at last awaken the people from their indifference. The bitter pain and fearful suffering will perhaps make a deeper impression than the words of the revolutionaries. It is possible that the Social Revolution will be the last act in the present tragedy; possible that murderous militarism will be drowned in the blood of its numberless victims; that the people of the different countries will unite against the bloody regime of modern Capitalism and its institutions, and finally produce a new social culture upon the basis of free Socialism."—"*Freedom*," *September* 14.

In an American contemporary a quotation is given from an issue of *Vorwärts* which was suppressed by the German Government. It reads:—

"The comrades abroad can be assured that the German working class disapproves to-day of every piratical policy of State just as it has always disapproved and that it is determined to resist the predatory subjugation of foreign peoples as strongly as the circumstances permit. The comrades in foreign lands can be assured that, though the German workmen are also protecting their Fatherland, they will nevertheless not forget that their interests are the same as those of the proletariat in other countries, who, like themselves, have been compelled to go to war against their will, indeed, even against their often repeated pronouncements in favour of peace."

TEXT OF LIEBKNECHT'S PROTEST.

The *Berner Tagwacht* publishes the full text of Karl Liebknecht's protest against the vote of credit by the Reichstag on December 2nd. The protest was not read, the President having vetoed it under pretext that it would entail a call to order. The protest was communicated to the German Press. Not one paper published it. It runs:—

"This war, desired by none of the peoples concerned, has not broken out in behalf of the welfare of the German people or any other. It is an Imperialist war, a war for the capitalist domination of the world's markets and for the political domination of important regions for the placing of industrial and banking capital. From the point of view of rivalry in armaments, it is a preventive war provoked by the German and Austrian war parties together in the obscurity of semi-absolutism and of secret diplomacy."

After declaring that this is not a defensive war for Germany, the protest continues:—

"A rapid peace, one which does not humiliate anybody, a peace without conquests, this is what we must demand. Every effort in this direction must be favourably received. The continuous and simultaneous affirmation of this desire, in all the belligerent countries, can alone put a stop to the bloody massacre before the complete exhaustion of all the peoples concerned. A peace based upon the international solidarity of the working class and on the liberty of all the peoples can alone be a lasting peace. It is in this sense that the proletariats of all countries must furnish, even in the course of this war, a Socialist effort for peace.

"But my protest is against the war, against those who are responsible for it, against those who direct it; it is against the capitalist policy which gave it birth; it is directed against the capitalist objects pursued by it, against the plans of annexation, against the violation of the neutrality of Belgium and Luxemburg, against military dictatorship, against the total oblivion of social and political duties of which the Government and ruling classes are still to-day guilty. For this reason, I reject the military credits asked for."—*From the "Daily News," December* 14, 1914.

"KARL LIEBKNECHT.

"BERLIN, *December* 2."

DANGER OF RUSSIA.

The following is the text of the resolution passed by the Central Committee of the Russian Social Democratic Party in reply to M. Vandervelde's appeal on behalf of the Allied cause:—

"We recognize the anti-democratic character of the Prussian hegemony, but as Russian Social Democrats we cannot forget another enemy of the workers, and no less dangerous—Russian absolutism. In home affairs this enemy remains what it always has been, a merciless oppressor and an unceasing exploiter. Even at the present moment, when we should have thought this despotism would be more cautious, it remains the same and continues the political persecution of the democracy, and of all subject nationalities. To-day all Socialist journals are stopped, all working class organizations are disbanded, many hundreds of members are arrested, and our brave comrades are sent to exile just as before. Should this war end in victory for our present Government, it will become the centre and mainstay of international reaction. . . . Our immediate objective should be the convocation of a Constitutional Assembly. We demand this in the interests of the same European democracy on whose behalf you appeal. Our party is a very important section of the world's democracies, and by fighting for our interests we are at the same time fighting for the interests of all democracies, enlarging and strengthening them. We hope that our interests are not considered as opposed to those of other European democracies which we esteem as highly as our own. We are persuaded that Russian absolutism is the chief support of reactionary militarism in Europe, and that it has bred in the German hegemony the dangerous enmity towards European democracy."

Letter on Russia from P. Kropotkin.

"'But what about the danger of Russia?' my readers will probably ask.

"To this question, every serious person will

probably answer, that when you are menaced by a great, very great danger, the first thing to do is to combat this danger, and then see to the next. Belgium and a good deal of France *are* conquered by Germany, and the whole civilization of Europe is menaced by its iron fist. Let us cope first with this danger.

"As to the next, Is there anybody who has not thought himself that the present war, in which all parties in Russia have risen unanimously against the common enemy, will render a return to the autocracy of old materially impossible? And then, those who have seriously followed the revolutionary movement of Russia in 1905 surely know what were the ideas which dominated in the First and Second, approximately freely elected Dumas. They surely know that complete Home Rule for all the component parts of the Empire was a fundamental point of all the Liberal and Radical parties. More than that: Finland then actually *accomplished* her revolution in the form of a democratic autonomy, and the Duma approved it.

"And finally, those who know Russia and her last movement certainly feel that *autocracy will never more be re-established in the forms it had before* 1905, *and that a Russian Constitution could never take the Imperialist forms and spirit which Parliamentary rule has taken in Germany.* As to us, who know Russia from the inside, we are sure that the Russians never will be capable of becoming the aggressive, warlike nation Germany is. Not only the whole history of the Russians shows it, but with the Federation which Russia is *bound* to become in the very near future, such a warlike spirit would be absolutely incompatible."—*Quoted in "Freedom," also in the "Manchester Guardian," October*, 1914.

The Future of Europe.

Portion of a letter written by P. Kropotkin to Mr. R. J. Kelly, K.C., of Dublin, December 15, 1915.

"The same for the South Slavs and for all nationalities oppressed in Europe. When the last Balkan War had shown the inner power of the South Slavs, I greeted in it the disintegration of the Turkish Empire, which would be followed by the disintegration of the three other Empires—Austria, Russia, and Germany—so as to open the way for two, three, or more federations. A South Slavonic federation—the Balkan United State was the dream of Bakunin—would be followed by a free Poland, free Finland, Free Caucasia, free Siberia, federated for peace purposes. Yes, dear Mr. Kelly, you are right, we are on the eve of great events in Europe. Warmest wishes that this should become a reality, or receive a sound beginning of realization, during the coming new year, and my very best wishes to you of health and vigour.—Sincerely yours,

"P. Kropotkin."

SERVIA.

"We are therefore justified in declining to accept such evidence. We are witnessing the birththroes of a new nation, the triumph of the idea of national unity among the disunited Southern Slavs, and it is the duty of Britain and France, whose Fleets are now operating on the Adriatic, to insist upon a just and permanent solution, based upon the principle of nationality and the wishes of the Southern Slav race. Only by treating the problem as an organic whole and avoiding patchwork we can hope to remove one of the chief danger centres in Europe." —*Lecture at Essex Hall, November* 13, 1914, *by R. W. Seton Watson.*

THE BATTLEFIELD.

"Then the camps of the wounded—O heavens what scene is this?—is this indeed *humanity*—these butchers' shambles? There are several of them. There they lie, in the largest, in an open space in the woods, from two hundred to three hundred poor fellows—the groans and screams—the odour of blood, mixed with the fresh scent of the night, the grass, the trees—that slaughter-house! Oh, well is it their mothers, their sisters cannot see them—cannot conceive and never conceived these things.

One man is shot by a shell, both in the arm and leg—both are amputated—there lie the rejected members. Some have their legs blown off—some bullets through the breast—some indescribably horrid wounds in the face or head, all mutilated, sickening, torn, gouged out—some in the abdomen—some mere boys—many rebels, badly hurt—they take their regular turns with the rest, just the same as any—the surgeons use them just the same. Such is the camp of the wounded—such a fragment, a reflection afar off of the bloody scene—while all over the clear, large moon comes out at times softly, quietly shining.

Amid the woods, the scene of flitting souls—amid the crack and crash and yelling sounds—the impalpable perfume of the woods—and yet the pungent, stifling smoke—the radiance of the moon, looking from heaven at intervals so placid—the sky so heavenly—the clear-obscure up there, those buoyant upper oceans—a few large, placid stars beyond, coming silently and languidly out, and then disappearing—the melancholy, draperied night above, around. And never one more desperate in any age or land—both parties now in force—masses—no fancy battle, no semi-play, but fierce and savage demons fighting there—courage and scorn of death is the rule, exceptions almost none."—*From Walt Whitman.*

Chinese Christians on the War.

"The most remarkable attitude yet taken in regard to the war by any body of people in the world is that of the native Christian Churches in China. I was told a fortnight ago by a missionary just returned from China that the Chinese Christians are holding daily prayer meetings to pray for peace. They are also praying earnestly that the Christians in Europe may be forgiven for killing each other, and, in particular, that the British and German churches and ministers may be forgiven for the blasphemy of praying to the Common Father for victory over one another, *i.e.* for Divine assistance in smashing and maiming and murdering more of their fellow Christians. I am also told that these Chinese Christians appreciate perfectly that for the most part the people to be killed are helpless, innocent workmen, who have had nothing to do with the cause of all the trouble.

"That action of the Chinamen is of the essence of real Christianity. It is the real spirit. It has been expressed in Europe only by the Pope, on the one hand, and, on the other, by the Socialists of the neutral countries and by the I.L.P. in England. It is the echo of the angel song of the first Christmas two thousand years ago. It is the true note, the eternal note. It is the note which will bring mankind back to its senses when the hideous passions, the false idealisms, and the sordid greeds behind this world tragedy are shown up for what they are."—*By Dr. Alfred Salter in "The Labour Leader," December 31, 1914.*

Essential Friendliness of Peoples.

"This essential friendliness, not between nations, but between people of different nations, is one of the biggest facts of civilization. And yet it has counted for so little that half the nations in Europe are fighting one another. Are the causes, then, that have set us fighting stronger still? Yes, when it is a question of national conscience. And one must regretfully say yes, as long as it is possible for those who rule nations and desire war to carry out their will.

"Is that wicked, mediæval power—in the hands of the few, but still strong enough to overrule the natural tendencies of peoples towards peace and friendship and to turn their likings into hatreds—is it going to continue when this war is over? Who can doubt, if it were possible to take a plebiscite of all the nations who are fighting now as to whether international disputes should be settled by war or arbitration, what the result would be? Is the desire of the many to have its chance when this war shall be ended, or shall we submit ourselves again to be dominated by the desire of the few?"—*From "The Daily News," October 5, 1914.*

"At one spot where there had been a fierce

hand-to-hand fight there were indications that the combatants when wounded had shared their water-bottles. Near them were a Briton and a Frenchman whose cold hands were clasped in death, a touching symbol of the unity of the two nations in this terrible conflict."—*From "The Sheffield Telegraph," November* 14, 1914.

Reconciliation in Death.

Letter written by a French cavalry officer as he lay wounded and dying in Flanders.

"There are two other men lying near me, and I do not think there is much hope for them either. One is an officer of a Scottish regiment, and the other a private in the Uhlans. They were struck down after me, and when I came to myself I found them bending over me rendering first aid.

"The Britisher was pouring water down my throat from his flask, while the German was endeavouring to staunch my wound with an antiseptic preparation served out to them by their medical corps. The Highlander had one of his legs shattered, and the German had several pieces of shrapnel buried in his side.

"In spite of their own sufferings they were trying to help me, and when I was fully conscious again the German gave us a morphia injection and took one himself. His medical corps had also provided him with the injection and the needle, together with printed instructions for its use.

"After the injection, feeling wonderfully at ease, we spoke of the lives we had lived before the war. We all spoke English, and we talked of the women we had left at home. Both the German and the Britisher had only been married a year.

"I wondered, and I suppose the others did, why we had fought each other at all. I looked at the Highlander, who was falling to sleep exhausted, and in spite of his drawn face and mud-stained uniform he looked the embodiment of freedom. Then I thought of the tricolor of France, and all that France had done for liberty. Then I watched the German, who had ceased to speak. He had taken a prayer-book from his knapsack, and was trying to read a service for soldiers wounded in battle."

The letter ends with a reference to the failing light and the roar of the guns. It was found at the dead officer's side by a Red Cross file, and was forwarded to his fiancée.—*From "The Daily Citizen," December* 21, 1914.

CHRISTMAS, 1914.

Letters from the Front (*from the Daily Press*).

"Last night (Christmas Eve) was the weirdest stunt I have ever seen. All day the Germans had been sniping industriously, with some success, but after sunset they started singing, and we replied with carols. Then they shouted, 'Happy Christmas!' to us, and some of us replied in German. It was a topping moonlight night, and we carried on long conversations, and kept singing to each other and cheering. Later they asked us to send one man out to the middle, between the trenches, with a cake, and they would give us a bottle of wine.

"Hunt went out, and five of them came out and gave him the wine, cigarettes, and cigars. After that you could hear them for a long time calling from half-way, 'Engleeshman, kom hier.' So one or two more of our chaps went out and exchanged cigarettes, etc., and they all seemed decent fellows."

* * * * *

"We had quite a sing-song last night (Christmas Eve)," says one writer. "The Germans gave a song, and then our chaps gave them one in return. A German that could speak English, and some others, came right up to our trenches, and we gave them cigarettes and papers to read, as they never get any news, and then we let them walk back to their own trenches. Then our chaps went over to their trenches, and they let them come back all right. About five o'clock on Christmas Eve one of them shouted across and told us that if we did not fire on them they would not open fire on us, and so the officers agreed. About twenty of them came up all at once and started chatting away to our chaps like old chums, and neither side attempted to shoot."

* * * * *

"I suppose I have experienced about the most extraordinary Christmas one could conceive. About seven o'clock on Christmas Eve the Saxons, who are entrenched about seventy yards from our trenches, began singing. They had a band playing, and our chaps cheered and shouted to them. After some time they stood on the top of their trenches, and we did likewise. We mutually agreed to cease fire, and all night we sang and shouted to each other. To cap everything, their band played 'God save the King.'

"When daylight came two of our fellows, at the invitation of the enemy, left the trenches, met half-way, and drank together. That completed it. They said they would not fire if we did not; so after that we strolled about talking to each other."

* * * * *

"On Christmas morning it was very foggy, so we had a short run on the top of the trenches to get warm. When the fog lifted we, as well as the Germans, were exposed. No firing occurred, and the Germans began to wave umbrellas and rifles, and we answered. They sang and we sang. When we met we found they were fairly old fellows.

They gave us sausages, cigars, sweets, and perkin. We mixed together, played mouth-organs, and took part in dances. My word ! the Germans can't half sing part-songs. We exchanged addresses and souvenirs, and when the time came we shook hands and saluted each other, returning to our trenches."

* * * * *

"On Christmas morning one of the Germans came out of a trench and held up his hands. Then lots of us did the same, and we met half-way, and for the rest of the day we fraternized, exchanging cigars, cigarettes, and souvenirs. The Germans also gave us sausages, and we gave them some of our food. The Scotsmen then started the bagpipes, and we had a rare old jollification, which included football, in which the Germans took part. The Germans said they were tired of the war, and wished it was over. Next day we got an order that all communication and friendly intercourse must cease."

* * * * *

"I went up into the trenches on Christmas night. One wouldn't have thought there was a war going on. All day our soldiers and the Germans were talking and singing half-way between the opposing trenches. The space was filled with English and Germans handing one another cigars. At night we sang carols."

Extract from a Letter published by the "*Berliner Tageblatt*" of December 24, 1914.

The author of the letter is Baron Marschall von Bieberstein, a captain of the reserves and Prussian "Landrat," obviously a kinsman of the late diplomatist and Ambassador in London. He wrote on October 18 from the trenches. He said:—

"Whoever fights in this war in the front ranks, whoever realizes all the misery and unspeakable wretchedness caused by a modern war . . . will unavoidably arrive at the conviction, if he had not acquired it earlier, that mankind must find a way of overcoming war. It is untrue that eternal peace is a dream, and not even a beautiful one. A time will and must arrive which will no longer know war, and this time will mark a gigantic progress in comparison with our own. Just as human morality has overcome the war of all against all; just as the individual had to accustom himself to seek redress of his grievances at the hands of the State after blood feuds and duels had been banished by civil peace, so in their development will the nations discover ways and means to settle budding conflicts not by means of wars, but in some other regulated fashion, irrespective of what each of us individually may think."

Unfortunately, the writer of this thoughtful letter fell on the battlefield.

THE END